Stan Fischler's
SPORTS
STUMPERS

Stan Fischler's
SPORTS STUMPERS

BY STAN FISCHLER

Assistant Editor
Steve Namm
Research Assistant
Alan Mann

tempo
books

GROSSET & DUNLAP
A FILMWAYS COMPANY
Publishers • New York

Sporting goods equipment on front cover
courtesy of Tempo Sporting Goods, New York City.

Acknowledgments

The author wishes to thank the following people, without whom *Sports Stumpers* could not have been written: Ira Lacher, Jory Levinton, Joe Resnick, Joe Pagnotta, Rich Friedman, Dave Rubenstein, Nancy Milholland, Robert Abramowitz, Bob Klepper, Mike Caruso, Evan Lipsitz, Karen Robertson, Ida Gross, and Kevin Kenney.

Stan Fischler's
SPORTS STUMPERS

Introduction

Al's Candy Store, on the corner of Nostrand and Vernon Avenues in the Williamsburgh section of Brooklyn, was, in 1942, the center of three major pastimes—punchball, association football, and arguing.

The punchball games took place on a rather large sidewalk just around the corner from Al's store. Association football, which I then believed was invented by Abe Yurkofsky who was two years my senior, was played in the street. Since World War II was in full horror, and gasoline was rationed, we had little fear of automobiles. Actually, it was the autos that feared *us*.

Our primary pastime, arguing, developed everywhere in the neighborhood but mostly at the counter of Al's Candy Store. Arguing was as much a function of a kid's life in Williamsburgh as breathing and eating. We argued over such philosophical questions as who was a meaner "bad guy," Adolf Hitler, Benito Mussolini or Hideki Tojo. Occasionally, we'd dispute the merits of malted milks made by Al and his wife, Shirley. (I always suspected that Al skimped on the malt powder so necessary to a good malted drink.)

Sometimes we'd argue over educational subjects such as who was the best teacher at PS 54. (Frances Hochberg usually got the nod because she made us laugh with her stories about Oompha-Oompha and Itchy-Scratchy.) Mostly, though, we argued about sports. There were two

1

basic categories of sports arguments—the emotional and the factual. By far the most consistent and bitter emotional arguments erupted over the merits of Peewee Reese (Brooklyn Dodgers) and Phil Rizzuto (New York Yankees), followed closely by the yelling and screaming over the best centerfielder of the day, Pete Reiser (Dodgers) or Joe DiMaggio (Yankees). To this minute, I still cannot resist the temptation to snap: "If Reiser hadn't crashed into the centerfield wall, he'd have licked DiMaggio on the best day DiMaggio ever had."

When the emotional arguers had railed themselves into a state of liquid butter (usually the time it took to consume one of Al's malteds) and it was obvious that nobody had won the argument, the boys switched to factual stumpers. The transition was often smooth because it was believed that if one could not obtain superiority debating the merits of Reese and Rizzuto one certainly could stump the enemy on a point of sporting fact. Thus, "Okay, wise guy, if you're so smart, who was 'Schuster The Rooster?' " Or, "If you know so much about baseball, which ball park has the shortest left field in the National League?"

My claim to fame at Al's Candy Store was the fact that I inevitably developed an affection for such unlikely teams as the St. Louis Browns, Homestead Grays (Negro National League), and Bay Parkways (Sandy Koufax's semi-pro team). This gave me a special advantage because I became not only an aficionado of, but also a student of, the obscure. Over the years my affection for the unknown and the underdog increased to the point where, in 1947, my favorite hockey team was the Sherbrooke (Quebec) Saints, which boasted the only all-black forward line in hockey history. Of course, I didn't know it at the time, but I unconsciously was doing my basic training for writing this book, *Sports Stumpers*.

My criteria for stumpers is simplicity itself: any sports question that can be legitimately answered by checking a record book or some authoritative volume on the subject in question. That, of course, eliminates the emotional stumper and the blooper stumper; the latter of which was immortalized at Al's Candy Store by one Joseph Vetere, who demanded of the throng: "Hey, who's M.L. on the Yankees?"

For several minutes the resident Yankees' encyclopedists puzzled over the problem as Vetere's grin grew wider and wider. Finally, the white flag of surrender was lifted over the malteds and the troops demanded: "Okay, Joey, who *IS* M.L. on the Yankees?"

To which Vetere triumphantly replied: "Mel Lallen!"

That's one stumper you won't find here.

Stan Fischler,
Boiceville, N.Y.

Which World Series-Winning Team Boasted a Creepy, a Coaker, and Two Coopers?

The 1942 St. Louis Cardinals. Coaker Triplett (along with Stan Musial, Enos Slaughter, Terry Moore, and Harry Walker) played in the St. Louis outfield when the Cards defeated the New York Yankees, four games to one. One of the St. Louis infielders was Frank A. J. "Creepy" Crespi, who played alongside Jimmy Brown, Johnny Hopp, George Kurowski, Marty Marion, and Ray Sanders. The Coopers comprised the Cardinals' famed pitcher-catcher brother act of Morton and Walker Cooper.

What Jockey Was Forced to Ride a Kentucky Derby Winner?

Isaac Murphy was forced to ride Buchanan in the 1884 Kentucky Derby. The problem was that Murphy had ridden Buchanan in the colt's previous race. During that race, Buchanan bolted to the outside and tossed Murphy to the ground. The rider was not seriously injured, but he was understandably reluctant to get aboard Buchanan in his next start, despite the fact that his next start was the Kentucky Derby. Murphy's refusal to pilot Buchanan left the horse riderless, and the stewards at Churchill Downs did not take kindly to seeing the horse scratched from the Derby for this reason. So the stewards merely informed Murphy that he would be suspended from riding for the balance of the

Churchill Downs meet if he did not ride Buchanan. Murphy was left with little choice but to climb aboard the horse.

Murphy must have regretted his decision as the horses entered the gate of the 1884 Kentucky Derby. Buchanan was fractious in the gate, and when the horse finally settled down, he got off to a slow start. But Murphy was unfazed, knowing he had a lot of horse beneath him, and waited until the top of the lane before asking him to run. From there, it was all Buchanan as he swept past the field and won the Roses handily.

Isaac Murphy did not need to be threatened to ride in subsequent Derbies—and he was to win the Kentucky Derby twice more.

Who Won the Boston Marathon and Then Caused a Scandal With His Post-victory Celebration?

Gerard Cote, April 1940. Armed with $17 in his pocket, Cote, the handsome son of a St. Hyacinthe, Quebec building contractor, took a bus to Boston and ultimately won the Boston Marathon in record-breaking time. Cote was so exuberant over his triumph that he celebrated the victory with a beer and a cigar. This demonstration scandalized the ultra-conservative Catholic church authorities in Cote's native Province of Quebec.

Apparently undisturbed by the furor he had caused, Cote won the Boston Marathon three more times, in 1942, 1943, and 1948, a feat unmatched by any other runner at the 26-mile classic. Cote estimated that he had run 138,000 miles during his 25-year career. He also set records in snow-shoeing contests in North America and excelled at baseball, hockey, and roller derby. As an added fillip, Cote also played rugby in England.

Who Was Considered the Brainiest Player in Pro Football?

Frank Ryan of the Cleveland Browns. According to author Jack Olsen, Ryan spent eight years earning a Ph.D. in mathematics at Rice Institute. "He blew one year," wrote Olsen, "trying to solve an unsolvable problem."

The scholar-quarterback led the Browns to a National Football League championship, but was continually pestered by newsmen over his educational accomplishments. Once, Mickey Herskowitz of the *Houston Post* asked Ryan to sum up his doctoral paper.

In response, Ryan scribbled a note: "It concerns a set of complex numbers which arises as limit values of a certain type holomorphic of function defined in the unit disk when the independent variable is restricted to an arc which tends to the boundary."

To which Herskowitz replied: "Thanks a lot, that certainly is simple enough."

Which Team, Pro or Amateur, Holds the Longest Winning Streak in Basketball History?

Passaic (New Jersey) High School, December 1919 to February 1925—159 games in a row. Although low scoring games were the norm in the twenties, Passaic's teams exceeded 100 points a game twelve times. One of its most one-sided triumphs was accomplished at the expense of a Stamford, Connecticut prep school, 145-5. During the streak, Passaic outscored the opposition by an average of 59.5 to 20.2.

Coach of this wonder team was Professor Ernest Blood, who was the third coach named to the Basketball Hall of Fame in Springfield, Massachusetts. He was preceded by Phog Allen of the University of Kansas and Doc Carlson of the University of Pittsburgh.

Although it was a high school team, Passaic drew huge

crowds. Once, 9,000 fans watched them play a game in New York. The streak was finally snapped on February 6, 1925, when Hackensack High School defeated Passaic, 39-35.

Who Was the Boxing Promoter Who Coined a Deathless Phrase for Baseball ("I Should of Stood in Bed") and Boxing ("We Wuz Robbed")?

Joe Jacobs. In October 1935, an ailing Jacobs was home in bed when he decided to attend the World Series in Detroit between the Tigers and the Chicago Cubs. Jacobs bet on Chicago but Detroit won the Series. When Jacobs returned home to New York and resumed convalescence, he told reporters: "I should of stood in bed."

Jacobs' other remarkable remark was delivered when Jacobs was Max Schmeling's manager. The heavyweight was fighting Jack Sharkey on June 21, 1932 when Sharkey was awarded a controversial decision that thoroughly enraged Jacobs. He rushed to a nearby radio microphone and shouted "We Wuz Robbed!"

Why Did Fight Manager James J. Johnston Invent the "30th Century Sporting Club"?

Johnston had been matchmaker for Madison Square Garden in the early thirties when a rival, Mike Jacobs, came along with a talented young heavyweight named Joe Louis. Jacobs promoted his fighter in opposition to the Garden and Johnston. But when Louis became a champion, the Garden was obliged to stage his fights and Jacobs took over as top fight boss at the Garden.

Jacobs called his organization "The 20th Century Sporting Club" (known to sportswriters as "Jacobs Beach"). Meanwhile, the still-industrious Johnston valiantly tried to maintain his stable of fighters and organized his own fight club. In order to "ten-up" Jacobs, Johnston called his organization the "30th Century Sporting Club." But Johnston's problem was that he lacked Joe Louis as well as enough talented fighters to keep alive in the business. While Jacobs thrived at the Garden, Johnston's 30th Century Sporting Club soon dissolved.

Who Had the Most Stitches in a Hockey Career?

No official statistics are kept on the number of stitches a player takes in the NHL, but if records were kept, it is quite possible that Eddie Shore would hold the painful distinction. Shore battled his way through a turbulent fifteen-year career from 1926-1940, spent mainly with the Boston Bruins. In fact, it was Shore that almost single-handedly gave the Bruins the "tough" image that has lasted throughout the years. It didn't take long for Shore to establish himself as a brawler, as he set a league record for penalty minutes in just his second season.

Shore shook off injuries that would put the average citizen in the hospital for months. In a single contest against the hated Montreal Maroons, Shore suffered a lacerated cheekbone, a two-inch cut over his left eye, a broken nose, three broken teeth, and two black eyes. In addition, he was knocked cold for fourteen minutes during the game. Shore did not miss the following game. In another incident, Shore broke three ribs after crashing into a goalpost. Instead of leaving the team to go to the hospital, Shore slipped away, caught a train to Montreal, and scored two goals the following night.

But despite Shore's reputation around the league as a villain (except, of course, in Boston), he was not your big, clumsy goon. Four times Shore won the Hart Trophy as the league's most valuable player, and he was a first team all-star no less than seven times.

Who Was the Only Known Professional Baseball Player to Apologize Personally to a Pitcher Off Whom He Had Hit a Single?

Archie Wilson, Toronto Maple Leafs. A balding, clutch-hitting left fielder with the International League's Leafs, Wilson wore number three on his uniform and liked to say it was "me and The Babe," as in Ruth.

During a game against Buffalo in 1954, Wilson came to the plate in the ninth inning with two outs against the Maple Leafs and nobody on base. The pitcher was Frank Lary who was one out away from pitching a perfect game, having retired the first 26 men he faced. But Wilson stroked a single to ruin Lary's bid. When the game was over Wilson, ever the sportsman, walked to the Buffalo dressing room and formally apologized to Lary.

For Whom Was Jackie Robinson Playing When He Broke Professional Baseball's Color Line?

Montreal Royals. Signed to a professional contract in December 1945 by Brooklyn Dodgers' general manager Branch Rickey, Robinson was assigned to the Dodgers' top farm team, the Montreal Royals of the International League. Robinson, who had starred for the all-black Kansas City Monarchs, made his professional debut in an all-white league on April 27, 1946, when he took the field for the Royals against the Jersey City Giants at Roosevelt Stadium in Jersey City.

At first the 27-year-old rookie was nervous. He grounded out in his first turn at bat and erred on a ground ball on his first fielding attempt. But in the third inning Jackie came to the plate with two men on base and whacked a home run into the left field stands. His confidence returned, Robinson became a scourge on the basepaths. He singled a few innings later, stole second, reached third on a daring sacrifice and scored after he induced the enemy pitcher to balk. He completed the game with four hits in five times at bat, helping Montreal to a 14-2 victory. The Royals finished first and went on to win the Little World Series. A year later Robinson was a member of the Brooklyn Dodgers, the first black to make it to the major leagues.

Who Made the Longest Shot in Professional Basketball History?

Jerry Harkness, Indiana Pacers, 92 feet. Some wild and woolly things happened in the heyday of the old American Basketball Association. One of the most amazing took place in Dallas during a game between the Dallas Chaparrals and the Indiana Pacers on November 13, 1967.

With just one second showing on the clock, Dallas' John Beasley hit a jump shot to give his team an apparent 118-116 victory over the Pacers in a hard-fought contest. While Beasley's teammates and some wildly approving fans were busy congratulating him, Indiana's Oliver Darden dejectedly retrieved the ball to finish the game. According to ABA rules, the game clock did not start until the ball was touched by a player on the floor. So the game was not over until the final buzzer had sounded. How many times have we heard that old sports adage?

While the celebration was still going on and Indiana coach Larry Staverman was heading for the locker room Pacer guard Jerry Harkness was standing bewildered under the Dallas basket. He moved off to the side while Darden inbounded the ball to him.

Harkness was an athlete playing on borrowed time since he was unable to make the NBA, having failed a brief tryout with the Knicks in 1963 after helping Loyola of Chicago to an NCAA title. In the interim period before the forming of the ABA, Harkness worked as a physical education instructor for the Quaker Oats company. When the ABA came into being he was offered a tryout with the Pacers and made the club.

12

As soon as Harkness got the ball from Darden he hook shot it as far as he could down the floor. The final buzzer sounded while the ball was in mid-flight and much to everyone's surprise the ball proceeded to go right through the hoop. In accordance with ABA rules, since the shot was taken from beyond the 25-foot line the basket counted as a three-point field goal, "the home run of basketball."

Harkness' shot, which was taken a step inside the end line of the 94-foot court, was measured at 92 feet, thereby making it the longest shot in professional basketball history.

Not only did Jerry Harkness make his phenomenal shot but he won the game for Indiana with it!

However, Harkness' amazing shooting feats were limited to one since he didn't have a good enough shot to stay in professional basketball. He drifted out of basketball and into obscurity.

How Did the First Rose Bowl Classic Come About?

A group of hotel owners and businessmen in Pasadena, California, decided that the town of 3,000 natives (in 1901) required some publicity. The promoters wanted to tout the virtues of Pasadena's mild climate in winter and decided to hold a Rose Festival on New Year's Day. In 1901 they decided to go for an added fillip—a collegiate football game. They invited the Stanford team from Palo Alto, California, and then sought—in an effort to stimulate an East-West rivalry—a team from somewhere east of the Rockies. The opening choice was the University of Michigan Wolverines.

Thus, on January 1, 1902, the first Rose Bowl game was played at Pasadena. In temperatures that climbed to the high 80s, Michigan ran up a 49-0 lead before the exhausted Stanford team asked that the game be terminated before regulation time. Michigan agreed. It marked the only time a Rose Bowl game was played in less than regulation time.

Which Hockey Player Was Assessed a Penalty While Unconscious?

Stanley Crossett was handed a penalty while out cold during his one-year career in 1930-31. Stanley was a defenseman for the Philadelphia Quakers who apparently did not listen too well. The rookie was warned about trying to split the Detroit Falcons' defensive pairing of Reg Noble and Harvey "Rocky" Rockburn, whose specialty was sandwiching unsuspecting attackers.

In the second period of a game against the Falcons, Stanley forgot the wise words of his coach, and tried to split the Noble-Rockburn defensive duo. Reg and Rocky, who loved to prey on green rookies like Stanley, caught Crossett with a beauty. Stanley went flying, and landed on his stomach and elbows. He slid all the way from center ice to the end boards, and was knocked unconscious by the ensuing collision with the boards when his stick was driven into his chin.

Meanwhile, Stanley had unknowingly gained revenge on Rocky Rockburn. While in midair, Stanley's stick caught Rocky over his eye, opening a bloody gash. However, the cut was worth a five minute major penalty to Crossett, who was lying unconscious on the ice. Thus the Quaker trainer led Stanley not to the dressing room but to the penalty box. When he regained his senses, Stanley had to be informed as to what occurred.

Which Nationally Syndicated Sports Columnist (Later to Become a Right Wing Political Writer) Lampooned the Coverage of Dog Shows on the Sports Pages of Newspapers?

Westbrook Pegler. A columnist who reached the zenith of his popularity writing a column for the New York *World-Telegram*, Pegler covered dog shows for five years and finally wrote what he believed to be the definitive putdown of the art in an essay called "Here Rover."

Pegler noted: "For the fifth year in succession I have pored over the catalogue of dogs in the show at Madison Square Garden without finding a dog named Rover, Towser, Sport, Spot, or Fido.

"Who is the man who can call from his back door at night: 'Here Champion Alexander of Clane o' Wind-Holme. Here Champion Alexander of Clane o' Wind-Holme'?"

Where Was Roller Skating Invented?

In The Netherlands. Sports historians have traced roller skating to the early 1800s when a Dutchman, name unknown, sought to find a warm weather equivalent to ice skating. He decided to try attaching wooden disks to shoes and, after a short period of refinement, roller skating became a popular pastime in Holland. The sport attained even greater popularity among the North American masses with the introduction of the steel wheel with ball bearings. A survey conducted in the late 1960s indicated that there are between 5,000 and 6,000 roller rinks in North America and more than 20,000,000 participants in one form or another of the sport.

Which Golfer Cost His Partner the Masters Championship?

Tommy Aaron, 1968. By the end of the third day of play the tournament had become a wide-open affair. At the opening hole of the last round, Roberto DiVicenzo, a relatively unknown golfer from Argentina, began making his move on the leaders. He eagled the first hole, birdied the next two holes, shot an even par on holes four through seven, and birdied the eighth hole. As the round unfolded it appeared that only two men had a chance to win by the 16th hole: DiVicenzo and Bob Goalby.

But on the final hole DiVicenzo bogied the hole when he

failed to drop in his short putt for par. Goalby had bogied the seventeenth hole and at the completion of 72 holes it appeared that Goalby and DiVicenzo were tied.

During tournament play in golf, when two competitors are paired together, they are required to keep score for one another. Last round pairings had DiVicenzo playing with Tommy Aaron. At the completion of the tourney each player is expected to sign his scorecard and return it to tournament officials. Once a player signs his card no changes are allowed to be made on it.

DiVicenzo was so delighted to be tied for the lead after bogeying the final hole that he failed to check his scorecard carefully. On the 17th hole Roberto shot a one under par three, but for some inexplicable reason his partner, Aaron, scored it as a par four. The scoring error incorrectly left DiVicenzo's final round score 66 instead of 65. As a result Goalby was the winner of the 1968 Masters and the owner of a new green jacket customarily given to the champion.

Who Did Bobby Riggs Play in His First of Two "Battle of the Sexes" Exhibition Tennis Matches Before Meeting Billie Jean King?

Margaret Court of Australia, Mother's Day, 1973. Ever since pre-World War II days, Bobby Riggs' name has been associated with championship tennis. The smallish native of Clinton, South Carolina, won the national singles championship in 1939 and 1941 and eventually went on to even greater fame as a professional. Riggs and Jack Kramer once staged an astonishing tennis match on December 26, 1947, at Madison Square Garden in New York. Despite one of the worst blizzards in Manhattan's history—more than 25 inches of snow had fallen before Riggs and Jack Kramer took center court—over 15,000 fans filled the huge arena.

Riggs, who was described as "the greatest money player ever to wield a racquet" by tennis writer John M. Ross, defeated Kramer 6-2, 10-8, 4-6, 6-4. Himself one of the most proficient tennis players of all time, Kramer paid Riggs the highest artistic compliment when he analyzed Bobby's game:

"The greatest weakness of good players," said Kramer, "comes in overplaying the ball, i.e., hitting it harder than they should or, in general, simply trying too tough a shot. *Only Bobby Riggs never overplayed his shots.*"

By 1973 Riggs, however, had been overshadowed by such young stars as Jimmy Connors, Ilie Nastase and several prominent women stars such as Margaret Court and Billie Jean King. Nevertheless Riggs, always a gambler, had an impeccable flair for obtaining headline-grabbing publicity and, in the spring of 1973, he boasted that he could beat the best female player in the world, even though Riggs was 55 years old at the time.

Before long Riggs' challenge was taken up by Margaret Court, who was the Wimbledon champion and a likely foe for the ebullient Riggs. They agreed to a best-of-three match which would be nationally televised and provide a purse of $10,000 to the winner. The loser would get nothing.

Experts pondered the question—how would the aging Riggs survive against the championship-sharp and considerably younger Australian star?

The answer was almost immediately supplied after Riggs highlighted the pre-match ceremonies by gallantly presenting Miss Court with a bouquet of roses. Bobby then proceeded to unmercifully rout his female foe in straight sets, 6-2, 6-1.

Riding the crest of his triumph, Riggs then challenged Billie Jean King, who had been U.S. singles champion three times and Wimbledon champion five times. Billie Jean agreed and the vigorous competitors met on September 20, 1973, at the Houston Astrodome before 30,492 fans and a national television audience.

This time Riggs was a victim more of his own overconfidence than Billie Jean's ability. During the month prior to the

match he admittedly spent considerable time partying and obtaining publicity for himself with all segments of the media. By contrast, Billie Jean diligently honed her game to sharpness and translated her hard work to the Astrodome court where she defeated Riggs, 6-4, 6-3, 6-3. Riggs' demands for a rematch—one which many critics believed would have gone in Bobby's favor—were refused by Billie Jean.

Which Baseball Team Played Basketball on a Stage?

The Brooklyn Dodgers. During the off-season the popular Dodgers frequently would seek employment in and around New York City, and once, to the delight of Brooklynites, they put together their own basketball team and played "home" games on the stage of the vast Paramount Theater in Downtown Brooklyn. Diagonally across the street a tavern was appropriately renamed The Dodgers Cafe.

Which Was the Longest-Running Musical Group to Appear at a Major League Ball Park?

The Brooklyn Dodgers' Sym-Phony Band. Baseball's zaniest musical combination, the Dodgers' Sym-Phony Band began their daily run at Ebbets Field in 1938 and continued performing until that sad day in the spring of 1958 when the venerable ball park was razed.

At each game the Sym-Phony occupied Section 8, Row 1, Seats 1 through 7 at the ball park and never failed to amuse friend and foe alike. Irving Rudd, who was the Dodgers' publicist during the halcyon days of the Sym-Phony, once described them thusly:

"They had a dual purpose: to amuse the crowd at the ballpark and to harass opposing players. There was JoJo Delio on the snare drum, Brother Lou Soriano belted the bass drum and was the Sym-Phony conductor. There was Patty George and Jerry Martin and Joe Zollo and his son Frank.

"The umpires, when they first appeared on the field to start a ball game, got the musical razz, 'Three Blind Mice.' When a fourth umpire was added routinely to every game, the boys were stumped. Complained Brother Lou, 'We can't help it. We cannot come up with the fourth mouse.' They used to toot and drum an opposing batsman, especially if he struck out, back to his dugout with a rhythmic cadence and waited until the player sat down, at which time they blared forth with a big chord. If it took a long time for the player to sit down, the Sym-Phony waited a long time, but the big blare always came as soon as the flannel trousers touched the bench.

"Back in July 1951, Local 802 of the American Federation of Musicians questioned the amateur standing of the Brooklyn Dodgers' Sym-Phony Band and threatened to throw a picket line around Ebbets Field. The Dodgers thereupon scheduled a Musical Unappreciation Night. Admittance was free as long as you brought a musical instrument. And so they came, more than 30,000 strong, with harmonicas, drums, kazoos and every conceivable type of portable instrument including—yes!—even two pianos which were brought into the rotunda at the main entrance.

"What a night for music! The weird noises unleashed by the capacity crowd of roof-raisers must have traumatized music lovers for miles around."

How Many Years Did It Take Vince Lombardi to Make a National Football League Champion Out of the Green Bay Packers?

The Green Bay Packers were among a number of "town" football teams that helped launch the professional game. Others included Rock Island, Illinois; Hammond, Indiana; and Canton, Ohio. The Packers, however, proved to be the only town team to survive in the big-league and succeed. In fact, the Packers remained a National Football League power until the late forties when a lengthy slump threatened the very foundations of the franchise. The man who saved the Packers and rebuilt the organization, Vince Lombardi, arrived in 1959 after working for the New York Giants.

Immediately, the Packers took a turn for the better. In 1959 Green Bay won more than it lost for the first time in a decade. A year later the Packers marched all the way to the championship playoff before losing to the Philadelphia Eagles. But in the following two years the Packers won the championship and the Lombardi era had arrived.

Which American President Threatened to Declare Football Illegal?

Theodore Roosevelt. Football suffered through some of its most difficult hours after the 1905 season. Protests had mounted over both the brutality and the high monetary expense of the sport. Northwestern University decided to drop the sport, and the president of the University of Michigan said he was concerned that football had taken on too much popularity on many campuses. More worrisome was the fact that an average of 15 to 20 players died each year from injuries suffered on the gridiron.

Such developments bothered President Roosevelt, who was moved by an editorial writer who described football as: "wasteful, wanton barbarity . . . not fit for humans to indulge in, or even witness." Late in November 1905 Roosevelt invited representatives of Harvard, Yale, and Princeton to the White House and warned them that football had to be cleaned up or he would abolish the sport.

Roosevelt's concern was translated into positive action by the university leaders. On January 12, 1906, a collegiate rules body was organized which eventually became the National Collegiate Athletic Association. Several rules discouraging brutality were introduced and penalties for roughing

also were added to the rule book. The President's inter-
ference proved to be a positive force for the collegiate game
and the excess violence soon disappeared. In time the collegiate grid game became one of the most popular in the
United States—something that might not have happened if
Teddy Roosevelt had minded his own business.

Who Was the Jewish Heavyweight Who Nearly Lasted Fifteen Rounds with Champion Joe Louis?

Abe Simon. A behemoth in the boxing ring, Simon possessed boundless courage. Despite his fortitude and size,
Simon was a plodder, and his bout with "The Brown
Bomber" on March 21, 1941, suggested a brontosaurus
going up against tyrannosaurus rex, Louis being Rex.
Nevertheless, Simon lasted 13 rounds before being dispatched by the champ. However, Abe was less successful in
a rematch with Louis, going down for the count in the sixth
round.

How Many Races Did Secretariat Lose, and Who Beat Him?

Secretariat was defeated five times. His first defeat came
in his very first race, a two-year-old maidens' race at
Aqueduct. Secretariat was sent postward at odds of 3-1, and
was under the services of an inexperienced apprentice jockey
named Paul Feliciano. The *Daily Racing Form* reported,
"Secretariat, impeded after the start, lacked room between
horses racing into the turn, ducked to the inside after getting
through into the stretch and finished full of run along the
rail." Despite horrible racing luck, Secretariat's late rally
was good enough for fourth place behind such undistinguished thoroughbreds as Herbull, Master Achiever, and
Fleet 'n' Royal. Secretariat's traffic problems out of the gate

caused him to be a bit shy at the start in the future, which resulted in his legendary rallies from far back.

Secretariat's second defeat also came in his two-year-old season, in the Champagne Stakes at Belmont Park. Actually, the Lucien Laurin-trained colt was first under the wire, but was disqualified and placed second. The *Racing Form* said, "Secretariat, void of early foot, settled suddenly after going a half, circled horses while moving leaving the turn, bore in bumping Stop the Music just inside the final three-sixteenths, was straightened up under left-handed pressure and drew away while being strongly ridden." So Stop the Music, who went on to become a good handicap horse, became the first horse to "defeat" Secretariat in a stakes race.

Secretariat's third defeat, his first as a three-year-old, was the most significant loss of his career at the time. Aqueduct's Wood Memorial is New York's major stepping stone to the Kentucky Derby, and Secretariat was supposed to have no problem. Sent off as the 3-10 public choice, Secretariat, as usual, was unhurried through the early stages. Big Red then "commenced to rally while outside horses on the back-stretch, continued wide into the stretch, lugged in slightly nearing the final furlong and failed to seriously menace the top pair." Luckily for the bettors, the winner was stablemate Angle Light, who was coupled in the wagering with Secretariat. But in second place, some four lengths ahead of Secretariat, was arch-rival Sham, who eventually broke down trying to defeat Secretariat again. Thus serious doubts were raised about Secretariat's chances in the Triple Crown races. As it turned out, the only effect the defeat had was to give bettors 3-2 odds on Secretariat in the Kentucky Derby, one of the betting bargains of the century.

After winning the Triple Crown, Secretariat went on to take on older horses in the Whitney Stakes at stately Saratoga Park. It is said that Secretariat was running a fever and not feeling up to par. For whatever reason, Secretariat could not cope with Allen Jerkins-trained Onion. After getting off to a good start, Secretariat moved to challange the pace-setting

Onion at the final turn. The pair battled head and head down the stretch in a thrilling duel, but Onion pulled away to win by a length.

In Secretariat's next defeat, the Woodward at Aqueduct, he again fell to an older horse, incredibly also trained by Allen Jerkins. This time, Ron Turcotte, Secretariat's regular pilot since his third race, moved Big Red into an early lead. But in the stretch Jerkin's four-year-old Prove Out moved up and passed Secretariat with surprising ease. As Prove Out went under the wire with a four-length victory, track announcer Dave Johnson exclaimed, "Allen Jerkins does it again!" Indeed, Jerkins, nicknamed the giant killer, had pulled off two of the most astounding upsets in racing history.

Of course, Secretariat will be remembered for his brilliant victories rather than his defeats. But his setbacks showed what the perils of the racing world can do even to the horse that many consider the greatest of all time.

Which Yankee Batboy Was Fired for Almost Killing Babe Ruth?

William Bendix, who, ironically, would later play the Babe in the movies.

When Ruth was at the apex of his career, a robust young batboy worshiped "The Sultan of Swat" and the Babe, in turn, encouraged the young man to pursue a baseball career. Babe's very wish was Bendix's command. The kid would shine the Babe's shoes, run his errands, and provide Ruth with all the food the heavy-eating Babe would require.

One day before a game, Ruth dispatched Bendix to obtain some soda pop and hot dogs. Dutifully, the kid returned with a dozen frankfurters and several quarts of soda. As usual, Ruth, one of sportdom's notorious trenchermen, devoured everything that Bendix delivered to the locker room.

This time the feast took its toll and, later in the afternoon,

Ruth collapsed with severe stomach pains and was rushed to the hospital. Headlines across the country proclaimed that Ruth actually was dying. When the Yankees' front office discovered that William Bendix had delivered the food to Ruth, the young batboy was summarily dismissed.

The Babe recovered and continued hitting home runs and drawing fans to every ball park in the American League. Meanwhile, the brokenhearted Bendix abandoned his pursuit of a baseball career and, instead, turned to the theater.

Curiously, Bendix played hundreds of roles, many of them involving sports figures. One of his popular parts was that of "The Bambino" himself, in *The Babe Ruth Story*.

Who Invented Spring Training?

Cap Anson, Chicago White Stockings, 1886. Following the 1885 season, player-manager Anson, a disciplinarian who implicitly believed in the integrity of baseball, became disenchanted with the off-year deportment of some of his players. As their paunches grew, so did Anson's boiling point drop until, finally, he read the riot act to his players.

In an unusual order, Anson instructed the White Stockings to report back to him almost two months before the start of the 1886 season. Rather than send them right out to the ball park, Anson took them to Hot Springs, Arkansas, on the theory that the famed resort would do wonders for their collective mid-sections.

Anson organized a rigorous daily training schedule, despite the complaints of his employes. But the man who is considered one of the greatest first basemen of all time was undaunted. He had led the White Stockings to five pennants and he was an extremely prideful man.

Although the complaints continued, Anson pursued his unique pre-season training program until just prior to the start of the 1886 campaign. Soon, the White Stockings began to perceive the method to his "madness." Their tummies shrunk and their muscles tightened. When the 1886 schedule was launched the White Stockings were in the best shape of any major league club and breezed to the pennant.

Cap Anson, who had startled the baseball world with his innovative spring training order, soon found that others were copying his pre-season program until, at last, it became very much *de rigueur* in baseball. Apart from the personal satisfaction that inventors inevitably obtain, Anson also was rewarded by induction into the Baseball Hall of Fame.

What Olympic Track Event Was Literally a One-Man Race?

Wyndham Halswelle was the only competitor in the 1908 Olympic 400-meter final. The 1908 Olympic Games in London were filled with arguments between the Americans and the British over rulings and rules interpretations. The biggest controversy was over the running of the 400-meter final.

Three Americans made it to the final—J.B. Taylor, J.C. Carpenter, and W.C. Robbins. Rounding out the four-man field was Wyndham Halswelle of Great Britain, who set a new Olympic record in the semifinals, blazing the distance in 48.4 seconds.

As the field broke from the starting line, Taylor, who recorded the fastest heat time among the Americans, broke slowly, losing all chance of winning. So it was down to a three-man race, and the field was tightly bunched as they entered the final 100 meters. Carpenter went to the outside to try and catch Robbins, who had a slight lead. However, Halswelle was also making his move at the leader, and there was contact between the Englishman and Carpenter. The judges immediately declared the race "no contest," and cut the finish wire before the leading Carpenter arrived. The Americans angrily contended that Halswelle could have stayed clear of Carpenter; they accused the British of voiding the race because Halswelle was beaten. But a rerun was set for the final day of the Games. The livid American officials ordered the Americans to not compete in the race.

So Wyndham Halswelle was the only runner in the 400-meter final. He could have hopped around the track on one foot, but he ran the distance in a decent time of fifty seconds flat.

Which NBA Team Chalked up the Longest Win Streak in League History?

Los Angeles Lakers, 33 games, 1971-72. On October 26, 1971, the Golden State Warriors defeated the Lakers, 109-105, and nothing presaged the events that soon would make Los Angeles a headline-grabber in sports. Five days after losing to the Warriors, the Lakers defeated the Baltimore Bullets, 110-106, and thus launched the longest winning streak in major professional sports. During their 33-game win streak the Lakers defeated 15 of the 16 NBA teams at least once.

The only team to escape defeat at the hands at L.A. was the Cincinnati Royals, which luckily wasn't scheduled to play the Lakers.

In compiling their remarkable record the Lakers were paced by Wilt Chamberlain, Happy Hairston, Jim McMillan, Jerry West, and Gail Goodrich. Surprisingly, the Lakers opened their streak after replacing perennial all-star Elgin Baylor at forward with young McMillan.

When the Lakers finally lost a game—to the Milwaukee Bucks on January 9, 1972—they had gone 70 days without a loss and had shattered the old mark of 20 consecutive wins established the previous year by the Bucks.

The record-breaking win streak catapulted the Lakers to the Western Division championship. They then continued their triumphant ways by defeating the New York Knickerbockers to win their first NBA championship.

Which Hockey Player Changed His Name in Mid-Career?

Because of their French backgrounds, many hockey players' names present problems for broadcasters. The recent influx of European stars into the North American professional ranks hasn't helped the situation. In 1947, a player named Enio Sclisizzi appeared on the Detroit Red Wings. Despite suffering a perpetual slump, Sclisizzi, to the horror of the Red Wings' broadcasters, stuck with Detroit through the 1951-52 season, although he missed the 1950-51 campaign, possibly out of sympathy for the radio announcers. For some reason, the Chicago Black Hawks acquired Sclisizzi prior to the 1952-53 season. It is not known whether the Black Hawks received bomb threats from the local radio people, but Enio Sclisizzi became Jim Enio. However, at this point there was no longer anything distinctive about him, and Jim Enio departed the big leagues for good following his one season in Chicago.

Who Was the Teammate Who Stopped Roy "Wrong Way" Riegels from Crossing His Own Goal Line in the 1929 Rose Bowl?

Benny Lom. A halfback on the University of California squad, Lom complemented the team's outstanding center, Roy Riegels. Playing against Georgia Tech in the Rose Bowl, California was deadlocked in a scoreless tie. During the second quarter, Tech fumbled and Riegels recovered the ball. Roy was immediately hit by an opponent but bounced off the tackle and ran free. However, Riegels, in caroming off the Tech tackler, failed to realize that he now was running in the wrong direction.

Lom was the only California player close enough to reach Riegels who was off on a 60-yard sprint. As Roy approached the goal line, Lom reached forward, grabbed his teammate's shoulder—while yelling at him—and brought Riegels down on California's two yard line.

Now California was forced to punt. The shaken Riegels delivered a poor snapback to Lom, whose punt was blocked. Georgia was awarded two points on an automatic safety. Tech scored a touchdown in the third quarter (but missed the point after), and then California scored in the fourth quarter and added the extra point. But Tech held on to the 8-7 lead and won the Rose Bowl. "Wrong Way" Riegels had cost his team the game, but Roy returned the following season and was named All-Coast center.

Which Racquet Sport Originally Was Known as "Poona"?

Badminton. Originally played in India, Badminton was called "Poona" centuries ago, but it wasn't until the game was imported to England that it attained international popularity. English army officers were responsible for the importation, having taken a liking to the game in the 1860s. By the mid 1870s equipment was delivered to Great Britain.

The sport got its biggest push forward—and its new name—in 1873 at a party given by the Duke of Beaufort. Since the game was played at the Duke's country place in Badminton, it became known as "the game at Badminton." Eventually "Poona" was replaced by one word— "Badminton."

Who Was the First Black Player to Win a Championship at Forest Hills?

Althea Gibson. Admired for her rapid moves and powerful forehand, Miss Gibson first made tennis history in 1950 as the first black to compete in the national tennis championship at Forest Hills. Although she lost to the then Wimbledon champion, Louise Brough, Ms. Gibson came within inches of defeating her accomplished rival.

But it was in 1957 that Althea would reach full flower on the center court. At age 30, Ms. Gibson routed Ms. Brough, 6-3, 6-2. Thus, Althea, in one season, became the first black to win at Wimbledon, to represent the United States in the Wightman Cup matches, and to win the national women's grass court title at Forest Hills. Curiously, once Althea's best tennis days were over she shifted her interest to the more sedate pastime of golf.

Who Scored the First "Grand Slam" in Big-Time Tennis?

Don Budge. In 1938 the native of Oakland, California, became the first player ever to win all four of the world's major tennis championships in the same year. No one before him ever held at the same time the American, British, French, and Australian titles. Budge also led the United States team to victory over Australia in its defense of the Davis Cup. In addition, Budge won the British and American doubles and mixed doubles. To complete the "grand slam" Budge defeated Gene Mako of Los Angeles at Forest Hills in the final round of the national championship by a score of 6-3, 6-8, 6-2, 6-1. Mako was the only player in the tournament to win a set from Budge.

Who Invented Miniature Golf?

Garnet Carter. A Tennessee real estate operator, Carter owned a small hotel near the summit of Lookout Mountain, the scenic Civil War battleground near Chattanooga. In 1927, Carter, an avid golfer, decided that his guests could use some added entertainment, so he built an abbreviated golf course on his abbreviated grounds.

Carter's idea became so successful, so fast, that he promptly began building courses all over Chattanooga, and all points South and West. Soon, miniature golf—abetted by

Carter's Fairyland Manufacturing Company—began spreading northward.

Three years after the first course was designed on Lookout Mountain there were 40,000 miniature golf courses sprinkled around the country, representing $150,000,000 in capital investment. Everyone, from Elizabeth, Queen of the Belgians, to gangster Al Capone was hooked on Carter's big-little sport. The only people who seemed *not* to like miniature golf were owners of movie houses. As more folks turned to miniature golf under the stars, they turned away from the cinema.

Which Teams Were Involved in Pro Football's First Sudden-Death Championship Match?

Baltimore Colts and New York Giants, December 28, 1958. According to seasoned football critics, the National Football League championship game at Yankee Stadium did more to boost pro football's popularity than any other single game ever played.

The Giants took a 3-0 lead on Pat Summerall's field goal, but the Colts went ahead, 7-3, in the second quarter. By half-time the visitors had built a 14-3 lead. Then, the Giants counterattacked, and by the fourth quarter had regained the lead, this time 17-14.

Although the Giants failed to score again they appeared well in command as the clock ticked away the final minutes of the fourth quarter. With 1:56 remaining Baltimore took control of the ball, but on their own 14-yard line. The stage was set for quarterback Johnny Unitas' heroics. Three years earlier, Unitas had been playing semi-pro at six dollars a game; now he had the Colts' fate in his hands. His opening tries were failures: two incomplete passes. But on third down he connected with a pass to running back Lenny Moore that was good for a first down. Unitas then ran off three consecutive passes to Ray Berry for 62 yards, and, suddenly, the goal line was in view. The only problem for Baltimore was that less than ten seconds remained in regulation time with the Colts on the Giants' 13-yard line. Steve Myhra was ordered to kick a field goal and he came through from the 20. Within seconds the gun went off with the championship game tied at 17-17.

Since the NFL had just ruled that, hereafter, all ties in championship play would be played to a finish the teams flipped a coin to decide who would receive the ball in sudden death overtime. New York won the toss and launched an offensive that fell short of a first down. The Giants were obliged to punt and Baltimore took over on their own 20-yard line.

Relentlessly, Unitas orchestrated a march upfield: a first down at the Colts' 40-yard line; then to the Giants' 42, and, finally, a first down on the New York nine-yard line. Unitas could have tried for a field goal but he elected to attempt another play. It was a short pass to tight end Jim Mutscheller that brought the ball to the one-yard line. The Giants were reeling and, despite a formidable New York defense, Baltimore barreled through to paydirt when Unitas handed the ball to Alan Ameche who put his head down and scrambled through a hole and over the goal line. The final score was Baltimore 23, New York 17.

Correctly Identify the Accomplishments of Either of the Two Sports Figures Named Tex Rickard.

The "original" Tex Rickard was a Texas-born promoter who came to New York to become one of the city's most renowned sportsmen. He was most prominently associated with boxing but also helped organize a group of financiers who built Madison Square Garden on 50th Street, the predecessor to the contemporary Garden. Originally the Garden, which opened in 1925, was to feature boxing, but it later became the home of hockey and basketball teams. The New

York Rangers were so named because of Rickard and his Texas background (hence Tex's Rangers).

A few decades later another Tex Rickard appeared on the New York sports scene. The latter-day Rickard was public address announcer at Brooklyn Dodgers' games at Ebbets Field and a character who became legend for his misuse and abuse of the language and attendant malaprops.

Rickard's gaffes occasionally caught the attention of the Ebbets Field multitude. Once, a visiting team complained to the umpires about coats and jackets which were draped over the railing in centerfield.

Dutifully, the umpire walked over to Rickard, who manned the public address microphone, and asked him to make a plea over the P.A. system about the disturbing coats and jackets.

Rickard obligingly took microphone in hand and intoned: "WILL THE LADIES AND GENTLEMEN IN THE CENTERFIELD BLEACHERS PLEASE REMOVE THEIR CLOTHING!"

Who Were the Participants in the Most Publicized Grudge Fight in Boxing History?

Joe Louis (United States) vs. Max Schmeling (Nazi Germany), June 22, 1938, at Yankee Stadium. Two years earlier, Schmeling, the pride and joy of Adolf Hitler, had knocked out Louis in the 12th round of the first fight. It was Louis' only defeat in his career up until that time, and it provided unlimited propaganda fodder for Hitler's claims of white, Aryan supremacy.

Determined to obtain revenge, Louis trained mercilessly for his grudge rematch. "He (Louis) was a big lean copper spring," wrote sportswriter Bob Considine, who covered the fight, "tightened and retightened through weeks of training until he was one pregnant package of coiled venom."

According to Considine, there were four steps to Louis'

first-round knockout of Schmeling. It began with the German landing his one and only punch of the fight. At this point Louis nailed Schmeling with a lethal left hook for the beginning of the end. Louis moved in and lathered Schmeling with everything he had, sending Schmeling, briefly, to the canvas.

Again Louis attacked, first with a left and then a right, and down went the German for a three count. But Schmeling recovered enough to regain his feet—for more punishment. Again he went down and again he rose. "He got up," wrote Considine, "long enough to be knocked down again, this time with his dark, unshaven face pushed in the sharp gravel of the resin. Louis jumped away lightly, a bright and pleased look in his eyes, and as he did the white towel of surrender, which Louis' handlers had refused to use two years ago tonight, came sailing into the ring in a soggy mess."

Tossing the towel into the ring was not acceptable in New York boxing circles, so the referee tossed it onto the ropes and began counting Schmeling out. At the count of five it was obvious that Schmeling was finished; it was then that the referee simply stopped the fight.

Curiously, Schmeling later embraced Louis in the center of the ring, but once the German reached the sanctity of his dressing room, he charged that Louis had fouled him. "That," concluded Considine, "would read better in Germany, whence earlier in the day had come a cable from Hitler, calling on him to win. It was a low, sneaking trick, but a rather typical last word from Schmeling."

When Was the Last All-St. Louis World Series?

1944, St. Louis Browns vs. St. Louis Cardinals. With all games played at Sportsman's Park, the Cinderella team of baseball, the Browns, provided the lordly Cardinals a large scare in the 1944 classic. Managed by James Luther Sewell, the oft-mocked Browns opened the Series with a 2-1 win over

STAN FISCHLER'S SPORTS STUMPERS

the Cardinals, although the winners collected only two hits off Cards' ace pitcher, Mort Cooper. In the second game, the Browns rallied to tie the game, 2-2, sending it into extra innings, but the Cards scraped together a run in the last of the tenth to tie the Series.

By now the entire country seemed to be pulling for Sewell's Browns, and they responded by taking the third game and a 2-1 Series lead with a convincing 6-2 win. But then the Cardinals' big guns began to produce. Stan Musial cracked a home run in the fourth game as the Cards triumphed, 5-1. Mort Cooper hurled a 2-0, seven-hit shutout in the fifth game, and Max Lanier got the win in the sixth and final contest as the Cardinals prevailed, 3-1.

Name the Popular Politician Who Was "Hired" to Reform Babe Ruth?

Jimmy Walker. Walker was a State Senator and an avid baseball fan at the time when Babe Ruth was hitting towering home runs for the New York Yankees. However, "The Bambino," as the sportswriters liked to call the home run king, liked to stay up late, drink whatever he pleased, and eat enough to feed a dozen men his size. As a result, Yankees' manager Miller Huggins threatened stiff punishment for Ruth.

At this point a group of baseball writers asked the persuasive Walker to attend a dinner for Ruth at the Elks Club and plead with the guest of honor to reform. Ruth, who had no idea about the behind-the-scenes machinations, applauded when Senator Walker rose to speak, but then the Yankees' slugger became stunned to the core by Walker's message.

"Babe Ruth," said Walker, "not only is a great athlete, but also a great fool. His employer, Colonel Jacob Ruppert, makes millions of gallons of beer and Ruth is of the opinion that he can drink it faster than the Colonel and his large corps of brewmasters can make it. Well," and Walker turned to Ruth, "you can't! Nobody can!"

Walker then pointed a finger at Ruth. "You are making a bigger salary than anyone ever received as a ballplayer. But the bigger the salary, the bigger the fool you have become."

Walker, who would later gain national prominence as New York's most flamboyant mayor, continued along this central theme until the mighty Ruth was reduced to tears. Finally, "Gentleman Jim" placed a kindly hand on Ruth's shoulders and said: "If we did not love you, Babe, and if I myself did not love you sincerely, I would not tell you these things. Will you not, for the kids of America, solemnly promise to mend your ways? Will you not give back to those kids their great idol?"

According to biographer Gene Fowler, Ruth bawled louder than ever and finally exclaimed: "So help me, Jim, I will! I'll go to my farm at Sudbury and get in shape."

Walker's diatribe worked. "The next year," wrote Fowler, "the Babe faithfully kept his promise to Jim, set a new home-run record, and at the close of the season was voted the most valuable player of the year."

The Ruth-Walker link remained tight, especially when the senator decided to run for mayor against the incumbent John Hylan. A tough politician, the aging and ailing Hylan attacked Walker for what he claimed would be the horrible things that would befall New York City if "Gentleman Jim" was elected to the mayor's office.

"Instead of replying to Hylan in the orthodox manner," wrote Fowler, "Jim met these onslaughts with full good humor." One day Walker was posing for a photograph with Ruth at Yankee Stadium when reporters informed him that Hylan had made a statement that Walker was the bosom friend of the underworld.

Walker glanced at Ruth. "Please don't steal any bases today, Babe," he said, "unless you wish to embarrass both of us!"

Which Basketball Star Played in 139 Consecutive Winning Games?

Bill Walton. Playing for Helix High School in San Diego, California, Walton paced his club to a 19-game winning streak during his junior year and a 33-game streak during his senior year. As a freshman at UCLA, Walton played on a frosh team that went 20-0. As a sophomore, he starred on the UCLA varsity, which won 30 straight, a feat that was repeated in his junior year. A year later Walton's team won ten in a row when he was sidelined for three games with a back injury. Upon Walton's return, the streak was stopped when Notre Dame defeated UCLA.

Who Was the Only Filly to Win the Kentucky Derby?

Regret became the only filly to ever win the Kentucky Derby, in 1915. The Derby was Regret's first start of the year. As a two-year-old, she was undefeated in three starts, all major stakes races in which she beat male rivals. Despite the long layoff, Regret was sent to the post as the 3-5 favorite. There had been speculation before the race that Regret would not run because her owner Harry Payne Whitney's brother-in-law was Alfred G. Vanderbilt, who was a victim of the Lusitania disaster. It was thought that the filly would be withdrawn in respect to Vanderbilt, but as the horses entered the track, Regret was the second horse in line.

Under the guidance of jockey Joe Notter, Regret took the lead soon after the start, and never gave it up. The only horse to mount a challenge in the stretch was Pebbles, who went on to finish third in the Belmont Stakes. Pebbles got as close as a half length, but at the finish line the margin was a widening two lengths. In addition, while Pebbles was feeling the sting of the whip through the lane, jockey Notter handrode Regret all the way. After the race, Regret looked as if she was just out for the fresh air; she looked like she could go around the track once more. It was indeed a convincing victory for the "weaker" sex.

Name the Boxer Who Won, Then Lost, Then Won Again the Same Bout?

Joe Giardello over Billy Graham, December 19, 1952 at Madison Square Garden. A Philadelphia-based fighter, Giardello gained a split decision over Graham, a New Yorker. However, Robert Christenberry, then chairman of the New York State Athletic Commission, was in the audience and believed the decision incorrect.

Christenberry ordered the ring announcer, Johnny Addie, to advise the audience that the decision was "unofficial." At this point, Christenberry altered the card of Judge Joe Agnello to favor Graham. Giardello's manager immediately protested Christenberry's move and took the case to court. On February 24, 1953, Judge Bernard Botein of the New York State Supreme Court overruled Christenberry and renamed Giardello the winner.

Who Perfected the Forward Pass?

Quarterback Gus Dorais and end Knute Rockne, Notre Dame University, 1913. Although the forward pass had been legal for years, it was hardly ever employed because few quarterbacks could master a football toss and most coaches were reluctant to "waste" a play by attempting a pass. But in the summer of 1913 Dorais and Rockne worked at a resort along Lake Erie and decided that they could make more out of the forward pass than anyone else in collegiate football.

Rockne believed it foolish for an end to simply run to a fixed position and stand still waiting to make a basket catch of the ball. He insisted that Dorais toss the ball over his head so that he could practice catching the pigskin on the run. They translated their workouts to the regular season and Notre Dame, then an obscure Indiana school, easily defeated its first three opponents. However, its fourth game was against Army at West Point in a year when the Cadets were one of the strongest teams in the country. Although the Dorais-Rockne passing combination had awed Midwesterners who had seen them in action, their exploits—partly because they took place against small colleges—were still unknown in the East.

Objective observers expected an Army romp. But Notre Dame held the Cadets scoreless for most of the first quarter, while deliberately refusing to try the forward pass. Late in the period the Fighting Irish's one-two combination swung into action—Rockne caught a Dorais pass over his shoulder and raced over the goal line for the first touchdown.

Army was stunned, to be sure, but not defeated. The Cadets counterattacked and took a 13-7 lead. Undaunted, Rockne and Dorais moved to the air again and their passes clicked. "This is going to be a picnic," Rockne told his teammates. "They just don't understand how to defend against the pass."

By game's end, Dorais had completed 17 of 24 passes, ten of them to Rockne, and Notre Dame had scored one of football's most notable upsets, 35-13. It took a tiny Midwestern school to make the forward pass on acceptable football strategy. Soon, Notre Dame became nationally known for its football prowess and, at the end of the 1913 season, Dorais was rewarded for his efforts when he was named All-America quarterback.

Who Was the Glamour Girl of Black Baseball?

Mrs. Effa Manley. As a co-owner of the Newark (New Jersey) Eagles, Mrs. Manley was beautiful and wise. According to author John Holway, who wrote *Voices From The*

Great Black Baseball Leagues, she also injected a touch of controversy into the sport. Although her husband Abe —older by 24 years—was the other half of the team management, players such as Monte Irvin figured that Effa ran the show. "She ran the whole business end of the team," said Irvin. "She wanted to create a lot of innovations. She thought they had to treat the ballplayers a little better—better schedule, better travel, better salaries."

After Jackie Robinson joined the Brooklyn Dodgers and then blasted life in the Negro leagues, Mrs. Manley harshly criticized Robinson. "No greater ingratitude was ever displayed," she charged in a magazine article after Robinson's tirade.

As more and more black players were admitted to the previously all-white American and National Leagues, the Negro circuits lost attendance and most eventually folded. In 1947 the Eagles' gate dropped from 120,000 to 57,000. "I lost $22,000 just to keep my team going," said Mrs. Manley.

Who Achieved the Worst Fielding Percentage in the Major Leagues?

Charlie Hickman, New York Giants, 1900. A butterfingered third-baseman, Hickman missed an average of nearly two out of every ten chances for an .836 fielding percentage. However, to Hickman's credit, he never committed nine errors in a game. That claim to fame belonged to Andy Leonard of the Boston Braves. Then, again, there was third baseman Mike Grady of the New York Giants who, in 1895, made four errors on a single ball.

For Grady, the problem started with a ground ball which he fumbled. As the runner crossed first safely, Grady pegged the ball over the first baseman's outstretched glove. The runner moved over to second, then dashed on to third. The toss to Grady at third was in time for the tag, but Mike

dropped the ball for his third error. This time the runner sprinted home and, predictably, Grady hurled the ball over his catcher's head for the fourth and final miscue.

What Was the Clumsiest Debut for an NHL Player in His New Home Rink?

Al MacNeil played defense in the NHL from 1955-1968 despite the fact that some observers thought that describing him as mediocre was being far too generous. MacNeil played for five different teams, and subsequently coached the Montreal Canadiens to the Stanley Cup in 1970-71. Despite the victory, Canadiens' star Henri Richard let it be known that he felt MacNeil wasn't much better as a coach than he was as a player. MacNeil was sent to the American Hockey League the following season, where he took over as coach of Montreal's Nova Scotia farm team.

Prior to the start of the 1966-67 season, MacNeil was traded from the Chicago Black Hawks to the New York Rangers. His Madison Square Garden debut typified his entire career. Leaping over the boards for a pregame skate, he fell flat on his face. Al MacNeil had forgotten to remove the rubber scabbards from his skates. The fall was an appropriate preview to MacNeil's Ranger career, which lasted one year, after which he was left unprotected in the 1967 expansion draft.

What NHL Referee Was Blind in One Eye?

Bill Chadwick refereed in the NHL from 1940-1955. Chadwick, who was inducted into the Hall of Fame in 1964, was totally blind in his right eye, the result of a freak accident during a game in March 1935.

If not for the mishap, Chadwick probably would have made a name for himself as a player. He was a promising twenty-year-old Ranger farmhand performing in an All-Star game at Madison Square Garden when the incident occurred. He was struck in the eye by the puck, and the blow caused him to lose all sight in that eye. Incredibly, he played for the minor league New York Rovers the following season, but called it quits after being hit by the puck in his left eye, although his vision in that eye was left unimpaired.

Chadwick's refereeing debut came shortly after his retirement, when the official for an Eastern League game got stuck in a snowstorm. From there, Chadwick went up the ranks —first a regular Eastern League ref, then an NHL linesman, and finally an NHL referee.

"The Big Whistle," as he came to be known, established a reputation as one of the most dependable refs in the league. He compensated for his visual handicap by making sure he was right on top of the proceedings. One would think that Chadwick would have been the victim of the players' sometimes cruel sense of humor, but he wasn't, although this was quite possibly due to the fact that no one knew about his blind eye. "In all my years I refereed and was an NHL linesman nobody said anything to me about my eye. If anybody had done it, I certainly would have remembered because I was very sensitive about it."

So respected was Chadwick that the year after his retirement, he was given a night at Madison Square Garden, where he now works as color commentator on Ranger telecasts. It would certainly take an extraordinary referee to be so honored again.

Name the International Sport Originally Derived from Vengeful Retribution of a Slain Warrior?

Soccer. According to *The Encyclopedia of Sport,* soccer (football in non-North American countries) has its origins in Great Britain. It has been said that the first soccer ball used in a game was the head of a Dane "who had been captured and slain, and whose head was kicked about for sport.'' The city of Derby, England, is often recognized as the birthplace of soccer, although Chester, England, also is mentioned. Derbyites claim that the first official game was held in their borough to celebrate a victory of a troop of British warriors.

Although soccer, in a primitive form, began to prove popular in Britain, it was banned on April 13, 1314 by Edward II on the grounds that it was leading to a breach of the peace. Several other lords of the realm attempted to sustain bans against the sport yet it proved too popular among the masses to be legislated against, and even William Shakespeare alluded to soccer (football) in his works.

In *King Lear,* Act I, Scene IV, the Bard alluded to the rough style of the sport:

"Steward: I not be strucken, my lord.

Kent: Nor tripped, neither, you base football player.

Lear: I thank thee, fellow.''

Again, Shakespeare alluded to soccer in his *Comedy of Errors,* Act II. The passage was written as follows:

"Am I so round with you as you with me

That like a football you do spurn me thus?

You spurn me hence and he will spurn me hither;

If I last in this service you must case me in leather.''

Who Was the First Indy Driver to Break the 100-M.P.H. Barrier?

Peter DePaolo, in 1925. Driving a Duesenberg Special, DePaolo roared across the finish line with an average speed of what was then an astounding 101.13 miles an hour! No one had attained 100 m.p.h. in the fourteen previous years of the race, although a team of L.L. Courum and Joe Boyer, also driving a Duesenberg, just missed the year before, at 98.23.

The feat was laughed off as a fluke by knowledgeable observers, who said that the automobile engine couldn't take the strain of 100 m.p.h. average speeds, and that DePaolo had been fortunate that his car had not overheated and stalled, or simply blown up. These observers apparently were justified in their smugness, for the 100-m.p.h. barrier was not broken again until 1930, and DePaolo's mark was not broken until 1932!

Which Famous American Novelist Helped Build Madison Square Garden?

John Steinbeck. Author of *The Grapes of Wrath*, the rangy, young Steinbeck, then an "unknown genius," carried bricks to the masons engaged in construction of the "new" Madison Square Garden, located at Eighth Avenue and 50th Street, during the arena's building days of 1924.

Years later, after he had become famous as a novelist, Steinbeck told friends that he got to thoroughly detest Madison Square Garden and never went near the place. "He told me," recalled one of Steinbeck's cronies, "that the Garden represented old backaches."

Who Was the Only Cross-Country Runner Ever to Get Lost in the Woods During an Intercollegiate Meet?

Anatole "Yanny" Levkoff, sports editor of the Brooklyn College *Kingsman*, also was a member of the school's track team. Levkoff disappeared in Van Cortlandt Park, Bronx, New York, in October 1955, during a cross-country meet. Eventually he made his way to civilization—an IRT subway station shortly after midnight.

What Happened to the Wimbledon Tournament During World War II?

It was halted because of air raids by the Nazis. During one blitz, the venerable tennis stadium took a direct hit and its center court was completely demolished. Legend has it that the bombing was an act of revenge perpetrated by a German tennis player whose entry into the famed tournament once had been refused, in pre-war days.

Who Was the "Little Miss Poker Face" of Tennis?

Helen Wills. America's first nationally known woman athlete, Miss Wills was so nicknamed because of her phlegmatic demeanor under almost all conditions. In 1923 she arrived at Forest Hills, a 17-year-old pig-tailed sensation, wearing a green eyeshade on the court that reminded journalists of newspaper editors for whom they worked. After she won the women's singles championship, she was soon compared with the French champion, Suzanne Lenglen.

A special match between the two women was held, amid grand fanfare at the French resort of Cannes in 1926. This time it was Miss Lenglen who displayed the aplomb, routing her American foe. After illness temporarily sidelined Helen, she returned to action in August 1927 when she defeated Betty Nuthall of Great Britain to win the singles championship at Forest Hills. By the time "Little Miss Poker Face" retired in 1938, she had won the Wimbledon title eight times and was known as "Queen Helen."

What Was the Best Put-Down of an American President by a Baseball Star?

In 1930, the first year of the Great Depression, Babe Ruth signed a contract for $80,000. The Yankees had rewarded him with the then astronomical salary because of his popularity as a slugger and value to the team at the box office. Still, $80,000 was more than a lot of money; it was outrageous. At least that was the opinion of one sportswriter who asked Ruth how it felt to earn more money than Herbert Hoover, the President of the United States.

Ruth, the Great Bambino, mulled over the question for a moment and then shot back: "Well, I had a better year than he did!"

Which Black Baseball Player Starred at Every Position?

Martin Dihigo. According to many observers who saw him play in the twenties and thirties for the Cuban Stars and Homestead Grays, Dihigo was one of the greatest ballplayers of all time. In a 1935 East-West all-star game, Dihigo started in centerfield and batted third for the East, and, in the late innings, was called upon to pitch in relief. Buck Leonard, himself a star with the Grays, and others call Dihigo the greatest ballplayer of all time. He was used at every position by the Cubans and the Grays, and in 1929 he batted .386 in the American Negro League. When the Negro National League folded and blacks began to enter the major leagues—by this time Dihigo was too old to make it to the bigs—he played out his career during the fifties in Mexico.

Which Team Was Responsible for Baseball's Longest Winning Streak, Yet Finished Fourth?

New York Giants, 1916. Managed by steel-tongued John McGraw, the Giants had come off a last-place finish in 1915 and were determined to make amends for their rooters in the new season. McGraw, the Captain Bligh of baseball, drove his team unmercifully to 17 consecutive road victories—an all-time record—but that still did not appease the bench boss. At mid-season he decided that many of his veterans had to be traded, and he dealt away such notables as pitcher Christy Mathewson and outfielder Eddie Roush.

On September 7, 1916, the Giants defeated Brooklyn and suddenly became a team possessed. A day later they met

Philadelphia in a doubleheader. Poll Perritt, who had won the first game for the Giants on the mound, pleaded with McGraw to pitch the second game after having been viciously needled by the Phillies. Demanding of his manager, "Let me beat those bums again," Perritt started the second game and came through with a four-hit shutout. Now the streak was for real.

By September 30, 1916, the Giants' undefeated streak had reached 25 games. Their next opponent—in a doubleheader—was the Boston Braves. McGraw's men won the opening game, lengthening their streak to 26, but lost the second match and ended their remarkable streak which had lasted from September 7 through September 30.

Despite McGraw's ranting and raving, the Giants finished nowhere near the top of the National League. However, they did enter the record books and, for that, they will long be remembered.

Against What Three New York Knick Centers Did Wilt Chamberlain Score Most of His Record One Hundred Points?

Darrall Imhoff, Willie Naulls, and Cleveland Buckner.

The 1961-62 basketball season was highlighted by the play of Norman Wilton Chamberlain and his Philadelphia Warriors super-team. Playing on one of the most awesome front lines in NBA history along with Luke Jackson and Chet Walker, Wilt "The Stilt," as he had come to be known, flipped, stuffed, banked, hooked, and dropped 50 or more points through opposing teams' baskets in 46 of the Warriors' 80 games.

As the '61-'62 season was winding down toward playoff time, Wilt's Warriors were assured a playoff spot and were on their way to posting what was then the best season record in NBA history. The Big Dipper himself had already estab-

lished a new single game scoring record of 78 points, erasing
Elgin Baylor's 71 point total. Never had the NBA witnessed
such an overwhelming offensive display.

On the night of March 2, 1962, the Warriors met the New
York Knicks in a virtually meaningless game in Hershey,
Pennsylvania. The Knicks were out of the playoffs and
without the services of starting center Phil Jordan. The hap-
less Knicks were forced to press journeyman center Darrall
Imhoff into action against Wilt, not exactly the opportunity
most benchwarmers would envy.

The game opened with the Warriors streaking to a 16 point
lead, 19-3. At the quarter's end, number 13 already had 23
points.

When Imhoff was forced to the bench with foul problems
in the second quarter, Willie Naulls tried his hand at stopping
Wilt. Willie gave it the old college try, but had about as much
success as his teammate, Imhoff.

At halftime, Wilt had already scored 41 of his team's 79
points and had the 4,124 fans in Hershey Arena buzzing in
anticipation of a record in the making. Things had been going
so well for Wilt that he had even sunk seven consecutive free
throws in the first quarter, a rare feat for the seven-foot-plus
scoring wonder.

By the third quarter, an exhausted Willie Naulls gladly
stepped aside for Cleveland Buckner, another Knick reserve.
His efforts were to no avail. Wilt was still surprising
everyone, including himself, as he shot a perfect 8 for 8 from
the foul line in the third quarter, upping his point total to 69.

Toward the end of the game a beleaguered Eddie Dono-
van, the Knick coach, was ordering his players to foul any
player, other than Wilt, to avoid the inevitable embarrass-
ment of a one-hundred point game. The New Yorkers tried
everything they could to thwart Wilt. Collapsing defenses,
stalls, intentional fouls all failed. With 46 seconds left to play
Wilt stuffed through his ninety-ninth and one hundredth
points.

In case you're wondering, the Warriors won the game,

169-147, thereby establishing a record for the most points scored in a game by two teams. That record wasn't even threatened until 1970, when it was equaled by Cincinnati and San Diego.

Wilt also established scoring marks for the most field goals attempted (63), most field goals made (36), most free throws made (28 of 32), most points in a quarter (31), and most points in a half (59).

How and When Did Skateboarding Come About?

In 1961 Californians, who made a ritual out of surfing, realized that they could obtain a *terra firma* version of the pastime by bolting skate wheels to tapered slats of wood. The surfers disdained handles to duplicate the "no-hands" feeling one gets on a surfboard.

By 1963 the makeshift skateboards were replaced by manufactured styles ranging in price from $1.79 to $14. No less than 700,000 people bought skateboards from one company alone, in 1965. However, the fad began to erode in the late sixties only to enjoy a remarkable comeback a decade later thanks to the introduction of speedier wheels.

Despite its innocent appearance, skateboarding became a dangerous sport. Deaths were recorded after skateboarders collided with autos and, in 1976, defenseman Pat Quinn of the Atlanta Flames fell off a skateboard and was so seriously injured that he missed a major portion of the 1976-77 hockey season.

How Did a Halfback Get Credit for a 95-Yard Touchdown Run After Having Run Only 53 Yards?

During the Cotton Bowl game between Rice and Alabama on January 1, 1954, Rice halfback Dick Moegle orbited into what appeared to be a certain touchdown run. However, Moegle completed only 53 yards of his sprint when an

Alabama player, Tommy Lewis, stunned the crowd by leaping off the bench to tackle the apparently home-free Moegle.

Referee Cliff Shaw conferred with head linesman Jack Freeman. They decided to award the touchdown to Moegle in accordance with the rule stating that: "The referee has the option of awarding a touchdown to a runner who is in the clear and is on his way to a reasonably assured touchdown and is tackled by anyone other than an official or a player on the field at the time."

Rice won the '54 Cotton Bowl, 28-6, with Dicky Moegle racking up 264 yards rushing on only 11 carries from scrimmage.

Tommy Lewis' self-attributed spontaneous reaction "twelfth-man" tackle created one of the strangest plays in college football history.

Which Sporting Event Resulted in the Worst Massacre in Canadian History?

A lacrosse match between two Indian tribes, the Sacs and the Chippewas on June 4, 1763. According to an account related by J.B. Patterson in "Black Hawk's Biography," the contest was staged near a fort named Michillimackinac, ostensibly to celebrate the birthday of King George III. Captain Etherington, the fort's commander, received word from the Chippewas, who resided in the vicinity of the fort, that the British were welcome to attend the Indians' game. But the correctly suspicious captain ordered the fort's inhabitants to remain inside the protected battlements.

Undaunted, the Indians suggested that the game be moved to a site near the fort, allowing the residents to "safely" view it from the fort. This agreed upon, the match began, but after an hour's play, many of the fort's residents believed that it was, indeed, safe for them to venture outside to obtain a better view of the game. Many of the soldiers, trappers, and traders who had been in the fort marched through the opened gates to watch the contest.

Suddenly, Michillimackinac was wide open, and totally vulnerable. Had they been more perceptive, Etherington's men would have sensed that something was wrong because the squaws, seated at the sidelines, were heavily blanketed despite the fact that it was a hot day. However, the naive British soldiers interpreted the blankets as merely a strange warm weather custom of the Indian women. Without warning, the players dropped their lacrosse sticks, sprinted to the squaws—who handed them the tomahawks that were hidden beneath their blankets—and sped toward the fort. The result was an unequivocal Indian rout. Only three whites survived, among them Captain Etherington.

Apart from being the worst massacre in Canadian history, the Michillimackinac attack marked the only time that a sporting event specifically was held so that the players could kill the fans.

Who Is the Only Known Person to Throw an Octopus on the Ice during a Hockey Match?

Pete Cusimano threw octopi onto the ice, and the lucky team of his affection was the Detroit Red Wings. Actually, it was Pete's brother, Jerry, who came up with the idea. It was playoff time in 1952, and the Red Wings had won seven in a row. Pete explained, "Before the eighth game in '52, my brother suggested, 'Why don't we throw an octopus on the ice for good luck?' It's got eight legs and that might be a good omen for eight straight wins." So on April 15, 1952, Pete Cusimano tossed a half-boiled octopus onto the ice of the Detroit Olympia, and the Red Wings won the Stanley Cup. Cusimano continued to litter the ice with octopi during each Red Wing playoff series for the next fifteen years. Of course, Cusimano's creatures have not succeeded in bringing the

Stanley Cup to Detroit in each of the years, but that did not deter Cusimano.

"You ever smelt a half-boiled octopus? It ain't exactly Chanel No. 5, y'know?" Obviously, Cusimano had mischievous intentions in addition to wanting to bring his beloved Red Wings good luck.

Which Champion Boxer Owned Teams in Two Different National Hockey League Cities?

Benny Leonard, who had been the lightweight champion of the world, bought the NHL's Pittsburgh franchise and operated it in the Smokey City as the Pirates with no financial success.

On October 18, 1930, the NHL Board of Governors approved Leonard's request to move the Pittsburgh franchise to Philadelphia. Ebullient Benny reacted as if he had been granted a license to coin money. He promptly spelled out elaborate plans for the "new" club, renamed the Quakers, and promised Philadelphians a brand new ice palace, which would replace the already antiquated Arena.

"The present building won't be large enough to hold the crowds," Benny boasted. "We are expecting a larger one to be erected three years from now. If it isn't, I intend to bring New York capital in here and erect a modified Madison Square Garden that will house hockey, six-day bicycle races, and wrestling."

Leonard's transplanted Pittsburgh club was nothing to crow about, either artistically or financially. As the Pirates they finished dead last in the American Division of the NHL during the 1929-30 campaign. With their record of 5 wins, 36 losses, and 3 ties, they were generally regarded as the joke of the NHL.

But Benny was optimistic about his team's chances in Philly. "I think ice hockey has the greatest future of any sport in America," Leonard predicted. "So I'm willing to risk my money. I've lost plenty so far but I'm not crying. It's the coming sport in Philadelphia and two years from now you'll say I was right."

The Quakers opened the 1930-31 season at the Arena on November 11, 1930, and lost 3-0 to the New York Rangers. They scored only one goal in their first three games, all losing affairs, before tying Ottawa 2-2. A momentous occasion —the Quakers' first victory—took place on November 25, 1930, at the Arena. The Toronto Maple Leafs were the victims, losing 2-1.

Leonard began to get the message, but his enthusiasm still ran high. "We're off to a slow start here this year," he admitted, "but I'm positive that Philadelphians will take to major hockey in another year or two. They have to become educated to it."

Leonard underestimated the Philadelphia fans. They were quite educated and were quick to realize that Benny had assembled what was to become the worst big-league team in hockey history. They did not win a single game from November 29, 1930, to January 10, 1931, and set a league record which still stands, losing 15 consecutive matches.

The NHL governors realized the depth of the Quakers' financial problems late in the season when the Montreal Canadiens decided to release defenseman Bert McCaffrey, who surely would have helped the Philadelphia blue line corps. The waiver price was a mere $5,000 and it was anticipated that Leonard would grab at the opportunity to bolster his team with an eye toward the next season. Instead, Leonard declined. Philadelphia had reached the bottom of the barrel.

Rather than departing the NHL in a blaze of glory, the Quakers made their exit in a pool of red ink. On September 26, 1931, NHL president Frank Calder made it official: Philadelphia had agreed to suspend its franchise.

Who Invented the All-America Football Teams?

Walter Camp. A member of the Yale football team, he played on the Eli squad from 1876 through graduation. He was noted for his shifty open-field running and ability to drop-kick on the run. He later went into the clock manufacturing business in New Haven but remained close to the football scene. At the 1880 football rules convention, Camp suggested the concept of the scrimmage line, to govern the positioning of both teams; the reduction in the number of players on a team from 15 to 11; and the designation of the quarterback as the man who orchestrated the offense.

Camp began selecting his All-America teams in 1889 and continued to do so through 1924, a year before he died. After Camp's death, the widely acclaimed writer, Grantland Rice, began selecting the All-America team for *Collier's* magazine.

Who Invented the Indianapolis "500"?

Carl G. Fisher. A young Indianapolis manufacturer, Fisher loved automobiles and was convinced that auto racing could be a popular sport even though in 1905 cars still were rather primitive in design and construction. By 1908 Fisher persuaded enough cronies to invest in a race track, and the speedway—which also would be a testing laboratory for the internal combustion engine—was built on a 400-acre field. He learned that the dirt track was the cause of dust clouds and decided to have the 2.5 mile oval paved with bricks —3,200,000 in all.

On May 30, 1911, the first annual Indianapolis 500-Mile Race was held and it attracted more than 80,000 spectators, the largest crowd ever assembled for a sports event in America up until that time.

As was the custom, each car, except for one, carried both a

driver *and* a mechanic. It was the mechanic's function to tell the driver when another driver might be approaching to pass.

But one driver, Ray Harroun, who worked for the Marmon Motor Car Company, decided to race alone. Instead of using a mechanic as his "watch," Harroun devised a rectangular mirror with a metal frame and attached it to the side of the auto body so that, by peering over the side, he could see his competitors behind him. Unknowingly, Harroun had pioneered the rearview mirror.

More than that, Harroun had one of the best cars in the event, which began with the explosion of an aerial bomb. No accidents occurred until the 12th lap when driver Art Greiner lost control of his Simplex and crashed into a wall. His riding mechanic, Sam Dickson, became the first fatality at Indianapolis. Near the home stretch the inaugural turned into a two-car race between Harroun and a car driven by Ralph Mulford. Harroun took the lead and never relinquished it, capturing the first Indianapolis 500 with an average speed of 74.59 miles per hour.

Who Was Called "The Lone Wolf of Tennis"?

Richard Alonzo "Pancho" Gonzales. A kid who grew up "on the other side of the tracks," Gonzales never seemed to erase the scars inflicted upon him as an underprivileged youth in Southern California. He remained a loner even when he had become the greatest tennis player in the world and toured with Lew Hoad, Tony Trabert, and Pancho Segura. While Hoad, Segura, and Trabert traveled together in spacious station wagons provided by promoter Jack Kramer, Gonzales drove alone in his own car, a souped-up Ford Thunderbird. "When the rest of the troupe stayed at one hotel," said editor-television commentator Dick Schaap, "Pancho stayed at another."

It was Schaap who labeled Gonzales "The Lone Wolf Of Tennis." Schaap, who knew Pancho in Gonzales' prime, offered a psychological interpretation of the tennis star's behavior, in terms of his powerful strokes: "Pancho is swinging at every Southern Californian who ever called a Mexican 'Pancho,' flailing at every tennis official who ever barred a youngster from a tournament, and whacking at every father who ever ordered his daughter to stop dating the kid from the wrong side of the tracks."

Gonzales was such a loner that he once had to be coaxed into posing with film star Gina Lollobrigida when both were at a New York party. While Gina wet her lips and smiled, Pancho scowled and snapped at the photographer: "Take the damn picture!"

Who Was Responsible for the Classic Baseball Boner?

Fred Merkle, New York Giants, 1908. Of all the turn-of-the-century baseball stars, Merkle was one of the least likely to commit a blunder on the field or at the plate. An expert first baseman, Fred could hit and he could field; more than that, he was regarded as an insightful tactician with few peers.

But Merkle's reputation took an irrevocable nosedive on September 23, 1908, when the Giants were playing the Chicago Cubs at the Polo Grounds in New York City. With only two weeks remaining in the season, the game was considered vital to both clubs.

The Cubs took the field with a 90-53 won-lost record. The Giants had 87 wins and 50 losses. The game that day reflected the closeness of the race. As the Giants came to bat in the last of the ninth inning, the score was tied, 1-1. It was late afternoon and darkness was descending on Coogan's Bluff, overlooking the ball park. The umpires held a conference and finally agreed that if the score remained deadlocked after the Giants' turn at bat the game would be called on account of darkness.

But the Giants were determined to somehow squeeze one run across the plate and appeared well on their way to doing so with two out and Moose McCormick on third and Merkle on first. Al Birdwell stepped to the plate and responded with a crisp single to right field, scoring McCormick with what everyone believed to be the winning run.

Apparently, so did Merkle. Having rounded first, the usually perspicacious Giants' first baseman watched McCormick gleefully cross home plate while Birdwell crossed first base. Instead of completing his sprint to second, Merkle stopped in his tracks and made a beeline to the Giants' clubhouse to join in the post-game celebration.

As Merkle trotted toward the clubhouse, Chicago second baseman Johnny Evers suddenly realized that Merkle had committed a giant blunder—he had forgotten to touch second base and legitimize the base hit.

"Gimme the ball!" Evers demanded for what was to become one of baseball's most controversial turnabouts, and he was given the horsehide.

With ball in hand, Evers stepped on second base and thereby technically and correctly forced out Merkle who never did reach the base. Thus, the winning run was erased and the game remained a 1-1 tie. However, fans already had swarmed on to the field in such droves by this time that the umpires decided to end the game.

Complicating matters for National League President Harry Pullman was how he should deal with the game if the Giants and Cubs were to end the season tied for first place. The president's decision was simple enough: in the event of a tie a one-game playoff between the Cubs and Giants would be held.

The Giants won their last three games of the season and thus closed the season with the same record as Chicago. The playoff game was staged—which New York lost. Baseball analysts promptly singled out Merkle as the culprit. Had he continued on to second base on September 23, 1908, the Giants would have won the game and, considering their outstanding play in the home stretch, likely would have won the pennant.

As it was, the Giants did win 11 of their 17 games in the stretch drive but Chicago won the pennant. The result was a total change in Fred Merkle's image. No longer was he revered for his hitting and fielding. Instead, wherever he went the fans snapped: "There goes 'Bonehead' Merkle!"

Who Was the Hot-Shot Collegiate Shortstop Who Became One of the Best Little Men in Pro Football?

Eddie LeBaron, Washington Redskins. A shortstop at College of Pacific in Stockton, California, LeBaron once caught the eye of New York Yankees' shortstop Frank Crosetti. After watching LeBaron field, Crosetti said: "He has the best arm I've ever seen on a college shortstop." But after watching LeBaron at bat, Crosetti had second thoughts about urging the kid to pursue a baseball career. "If I were you, kid," Crosetti advised, "I'd stick to football."

LeBaron's problem was that he stood 5-7, 165 pounds, but his talent was immense and, in 1950, the Washington Redskins signed Eddie to a contract. When the rookie showed up at the Redskins' camp, a newspaperman looked him over as LeBaron disappeared into a huddle and joked: "Good heavens, the kid won't see the sun all season!"

LeBaron ultimately became one of pro football's finest quarterbacks, and in 1958 he had become the number one passer in the country. Mike Nixon, who had been LeBaron's coach for a few seasons in Washington, said of Eddie: "When I first saw him, I was sure he was too small, but now I've seen him do things I thought were impossible and do them again and again until they became routine."

What Was the Greatest Nickname for a Hockey Club?

The Macon (Georgia) Whoopies. Strange as it may seem, the Whoopies not only were a hockey team, but they played in a real, live professional unit, the Southern League. That is, they did for a short while. Very short. Many people, including a man named Robert Fierro, believed the Macon Whoopies never should have been created.

A hockey fan, Fierro, who once was a public relations consultant, had worked with a chap named Gerald C. Pinkerton, a financial consultant, in organizing the Southern League. The league was launched with teams from Charlotte, Greensboro, Roanoke, St. Petersburg, and Winston-Salem.

Somehow, a sixth city was deemed necessary to round out the circuit and Macon, a molasses-slow town 60 miles from Atlanta, was chosen.

Southern League governors urged Pinkerton to take the team, but he declined. However, a phone conversation with Fierro turned things around. The dialogue went like this:

"They want me to buy a hockey team," said Pinkerton.

"So?" countered Fierro.

"What am I going to do with a hockey team?"

"Look, you've always wanted to be in sports. You're a hockey nut. The fact that you aren't rich shouldn't hinder you. Form a syndicate. Buy the damn team."

"In Macon?"

"Why not? You could always call them the *Macon Whoopies!*"

Fierro swears that that's exactly how the club name came into being. It turned out that Pinkerton's favorite song was Doris Day's recording of the Gus Kahn classic tune, "Makin' Whoopie!"

Pinkerton still wasn't sure he should get into hockey. He turned to his neighbor at the bar for advice. The neighbor happened to be Tim Ryan, then NBC's play-by-play broadcaster for the "NHL Game of the Week."

"If you had a hockey team," asked Pinkerton, "in Macon, Georgia, what would you name them?"

"I like the Macon Eggs," Ryan shot back.

"Would you believe the Macon Whoopies?" snapped Pinkerton.

Ryan's eyes lit up. "If you do *that* I'll give your scores on the air every week and make you the Slippery Rock of hockey."

Pinkerton was sold on the idea. So, he bought the team and named them the Whoopies.

Everybody, from local newscasters to the city fathers, loved the Whoopies. So did the *Wall Street Journal* and *Sports Illustrated,* each of which mentioned the team with affection, as did the national wire services. The whole hockey world, it seemed, was ga-ga over the Whoopies. The only trouble was, nobody went to see them at the 7,500-seat Coliseum.

The Whoopies remained in second place for most of the first half of the season, although the players frequently didn't get paid (attendance averaged only 1,100) and the promotion manager suffered a nervous breakdown brought on by malnutrition.

The end was in sight and, finally, in February 1974, the Macon Whoopies played their final game.

"The ice melted," said Fierro, "and so did a lot of wallets, mine included. There was lots of whoopie in Macon, but there was no makin' money!"

Name the Only Triple-Threat Brother Act in Basketball and Hockey Broadcasting?

Marv, Al, and Steve Albert. The Brooklyn-born Albert brothers have covered nearly all of the major professional sports. Marv, the oldest, began his career as a ball-boy for the New York Knickerbockers and, eventually, became play-by-play broadcaster for the Knicks, Rangers, and Football Giants. Al, the second oldest, was the play-by-play radio broadcaster and, later, telecaster for the New York Islanders and Nets before heading west to become play-by-play man for the Denver Nuggets. The youngest Albert, Steve, followed Al's footsteps and handled both Nets and Islanders games before becoming a CBS-TV sportscaster in the spring of 1977. How did it happen? Marv once explained:

"When Al, Steve, and I weren't watching the big-leaguers, we were organizing our own games in front of our house. Armed with a tape recorder and a microphone, one of us would handle play-by-play as if we were right up there in the big-time." Eventually, they all made it to the top.

During the Same Week that Columnist Grantland Rice Created the Nickname "The Four Horsemen," Another Football Event Was Taking Place that Would Inspire Rice to Coin Still Another Nickname. What Was the Event and Who Was Nicknamed?

The University of Illinois defeated greatly favored Michigan, 39-14 as Red Grange carried the ball 21 times for 402 yards. Grantland Rice was at the Notre Dame-Army game halfway across the country, where Stuhldreher, Miller, Crowley, and Layden—The Four Horsemen—helped defeat Army, 13-7. But Rice was so moved upon hearing of Grange and the Illinois upset over Michigan that he wrote the following verse in his column:

A streak of fire, a breath of flame,
  Eluding all who reach and clutch;
A gray ghost thrown into the game,
  That rival hands may seldom touch.

From then on Red Grange came to be known as football's "Galloping Ghost."

When Jackie Robinson Broke the "Color Line" with the Montreal Royals in April 1946 the Royals Had a Second Black Man on Their Roster. Who Was He?

John Wright, a 27-year-old right-handed pitcher. Prior to signing with the Brooklyn Dodgers' organization, Wright had starred with the Newark Eagles, Pittsburgh Crawfords, and Homestead Grays. While Robinson was an instant International League star, Wright made only two appearances in relief for the Royals before being optioned to Three Rivers, Quebec in the Class-C Border League. He finished the season there and was unconditionally released by the Dodgers' organization that winter and returned to the Homestead Grays.

Why did Robinson succeed and Wright fail? Robinson once explained: "John had all the ability in the world, as far as physical abilities were concerned. But John couldn't stand the pressure of going up into this new league and being one of the first. The things that went on up there were too much for him, and John was not able to perform up to his capabilities.

"In a number of cities, we had very little pressure. But there was always that little bit coming out. It wasn't so much based on race—I think most of the Negro players could have done it as far as race. But because John was the first Negro pitcher, every time he stepped out there he seemed to lose that fineness, and he tried a little bit harder than he was capable of playing. He tried to do more than he was able to do, and it caused him to be a lot less of a pitcher than he actually was. If he had come in two or three years later when the pressure was off, John could have made it in the major leagues."

When Wright was optioned out in May 1946 the Royals added another black pitcher, Roy Partlow, a 30-year-old. But later in the season he too was optioned to Three Rivers. Thus, Robinson was the only black player to survive the entire season with the Royals. Meanwhile, the Dodgers signed Roy Campanella, who had starred for the Baltimore Elite Giants, and Don Newcombe, a pitcher with the Newark Eagles, and assigned both to Nashua in the Class B New England League.

Liberty Island Was the Site of Which Famous Race Prior to Miss Liberty's Appearance There?

In July 1851 what has come to be regarded as the most famous sculling race of the 19th century was held in the waters off New York City. The participants were James Lee and William Decker, who agreed to race for a side bet of $900. However, by race time, it was estimated that more than $100,000 was bet by onlookers. The five-mile course circled Bedloes Island, eventually to where the Statue of Liberty now stands. Decker won the race by a fifth of a mile.

What Is the Difference between Ping Pong and Table Tennis?

Ping Pong and table tennis are different names for the same game. Technically, Ping Pong is an incorrect description of table tennis since Ping Pong was a commercial name given to the sport by the London, England sporting equipment company, Hamley Brothers. The firm had become the British distributor for Parker Brothers, a sports equipment manufacturing concern, which originally called the game "Indoor Tennis." However, the Hamleys, likening the "ping" for the sound that resulted from the racquet hitting the ball and "pong" for the ball hitting the table, decided to popularize the game by giving it the name Ping Pong. Sensing that the public accepted the catchy name, Parker Brothers patented the words "Ping Pong" both in Britain and the United States. However, the sport became so popular by the twenties that copyright problems over the use of Ping Pong as the sport's name became so numerous that it was officially dubbed "table tennis" and was ruled by the International Table Tennis Federation.

What Is a Skeet and Why Do People Shoot It?

Skeet shooting is a sport that came about as a refinement of the English pastime of trap shooting. Using the same clay "birds" employed in trapshooting, skeet shooting originally was called "Round the Clock Shooting" because shots were fired to all points of the compass. The name skeet shooting was provided as a result of a contest held by *National Sportsman* magazine. After 10,000 entries were considered, "skeet" was selected and Mrs. Gertrude Hurlbutt of Dayton, Montana was awarded the $100 for the suggestion. She explained that she chose the word "skeet" because it was a Scandinavian word meaning "shoot." During skeet shooting, guns are directed at targets as they are in trap shooting. The "skeet," saucer-shaped, supposedly equals the swift, steady flight of a quail once it is aloft.

Who Was the First College Basketball Player to Score Over 1,000 Points in a Season?

Johnny O'Brien, Seattle University, 1951-52. Johnny was one half of a twin-brother backcourt, along with Eddie. The two South Amboy, New Jersey, products were both listed as a diminuitive 5'9", although Eddie was really a half-inch shorter. Johnny O was a prolific scorer; besides being a dead-aim jump shooter, he was also able to penetrate and go to the hoop. Many of Johnny's buckets were set up by his brother, whose main job was to do just that.

The O'Briens were Seattle's starting guards for their entire four years there. Johnny O scored over 500 points as a freshman. The following year, playing without an injured Eddie for six weeks, Johnny scored 766 points, at a 20.7 per game clip, in leading the Chieftans to a 32-5 record.

But it was in his junior year that Johnny achieved national prominence by shattering the old single season scoring mark of 967 points, and becoming the first college player to score over 1,000 points, finishing with 1,051. He averaged a productive 28.4 points per ball game. Johnny also placed sixth in the nation in field-goal accuracy, an incredible achievement for a 5'9" guard.

After leading Seattle to the NCAA tournament in their senior year, the twins went on to form a rookie double-play combo for the 1953 Pittsburgh Pirates. Upon returning from a year in the armed forces, Johnny batted .299 as the Pirates' second baseman in 1955, but was soon replaced by a great prospect named Bill Mazeroski.

Which National Football League Players Were the Victims of Gratituitous Violence Early in the 1976 Season?

Cheap shots have been an obsession with National Football League players for many years. Without discrimination, pass receivers and running backs get them, and cornerbacks and linebackers give them. One maxim holds fast in the NFL: "It is better to give than to receive." But, in some cases, the giver is liable to get something in return.

Dirty tactics on the gridiron received a lot of ink during the 1976 NFL season as the result of crippling injuries to several quarterbacks, receivers, and runners. The furor began on opening day, when the world champion Pittsburgh Steelers renewed their hate campaign with the Oakland Raiders at Oakland's Alameda County Stadium.

During the contest Pittsburgh's splendid receiver Lynn Swann absorbed two separate, vicious hits on pass plays; one by Oakland defensive back Jack Tatum which knocked him dizzy and a karate-type forearm smash on the back of the head by another defensive back, George Atkinson.

Atkinson's hit provided Swann with a concussion, forcing him to leave the game. "It wasn't until I hit him that I saw that Franco Harris (Steeler running back) had the ball," Atkinson stated afterwards. "I wasn't trying to hurt him, but I have no regrets."

Steelers' head coach Chuck Noll was furious with the Raiders' "game plan," and criticized them for representing "a criminal element." The "criminals" received their penalties a week later when Commissioner Pete Rozelle fined Tatum $750 and then slapped Atkinson with a $1,500 fine. Noll was fined $1,200 because of a rule in the NFL's constitution prohibiting public criticism of other teams.

Some overzealous hitting instigated fisticuffs—or *fingercuffs*—exactly three weeks after the Swann concussion. The Houston Oilers were leading the New Orleans Saints, 31-16, in the fourth quarter of their game in the Louisiana Superdome. Despite the fact that rookie wide receiver Tinker Owens of the home town Saints had already made three receptions for 96 yards and a 60-yard touchdown catch, Houston cornerback Zeke Moore, who Owens beat on the TD, now was attempting to make an unauthorized withdrawal.

Curiously, Owens wasn't even involved directly in the play on which Moore was trying to get even. New Orleans quarterback Bobby Douglass had completed a pass to running back Tony Galbreath, who carried the ball 17 yards for a first down to the Houston 25-yard line before being wrestled down hard by linebacker Ted Washington. Owens was blocking for Galbreath on the play and was bumped hard out-of-bounds by Moore, who wasn't involved with the tackle. As the whistle blew to stop the clock, Moore bumped Owens a second time, only harder.

The rookie, not yet acclimated to the viciousness of NFL football, became riled and took a swing at Moore. Both benches then emptied onto the field and the game eventually was delayed for about ten minutes.

Things cooled off for a few moments, until Owens and Moore started walking, side by side, back to their respective huddles. But they weren't exactly holding hands. "We were walking along," says Owens, "and he was telling me how he was going to get me. I looked at him and said, 'We'll see,' or something like that; and then he threw those fingers."

The Oilers' defender wanted to hit Owens with his fist, but it was too large to fit through Tinker's helmet. So, instead, Moore took two fingers and poked him in the eye, a la Moe Howard. According to Saints' public relations director Harry Hulmes, Owens fell to the ground "like he was poleaxed."

As the injured Saint lay quivering on the artificial turf in front of the New Orleans bench, his stunned and angry teammates rushed the officials to complain about Moore's cheap shot. Quarterback Archie Manning, who was on the bench injured, pushed the referee during the argument and was ejected; likewise Saints' tight end Paul Seal, who also beefed long and loudly to the officials.

Even John Mecom Jr., the Saints' owner, got into the act and was fined $5,000 for being on the field and arguing with the Oilers' assistant coach Ed Biles. While Tinker Owens was being wheeled away on a stretcher, the officials confered for several minutes before ejecting Moore from the game. Manning was subsequently fined $500 and Seal was relieved of $250. Zeke Moore wasn't fined a cent.

Which Golfer Played Despite a Chronic Ailment?

Byron Nelson, one of America's greatest golfers (winner of 19 tournaments in 1945 and eleven in a row that same year) played despite a case of hemophilia, the so-called "bleeder's disease." His career was short but illustrious.

Prize-Winning Author Sinclair Lewis Described the Meaning of Baseball to America in Which Famous Book?

Babbitt. The excerpt went as follows:

"A sensational event was changing from the brown suit to the gray the contents of his pockets. He was earnest about these objects. They were of eternal importance, like baseball or the Republican Party."

Why Did the Houston Astros Install Artificial Turf at the Astrodome?

It wasn't planned that way. Originally, grass grew under the Texas dome, bathed in brilliant sunlight. However, when outfielders began complaining about the glare, the dome was painted opaque. Unfortunately, the grass then stopped growing. The only alternative was the installation of artificial turf, which had just been developed by the Monsanto Corporation. Thus, the "grass" that revolutionized baseball!

Who Was Bill "Moose" Skowron's Defensive Replacement When Skowron Played for the New York Yankees?

It was Marvin Eugene Throneberry, the "Marvelous Marv" of New York Mets infamy. Manager Casey Stengel used Marv to replace Skowron in the late innings because Skowron's glove was notoriously porous. Of course Marv, who established his fame as a Met, never challenged for a "Golden Glove" either. But the fact remains that Throneberry started his major league career as a defensive specialist.

Which Ball Park Boasted the Most Difficult "Hit Sign, Win Suit" Sign in the Major Leagues?

Ebbets Field, Brooklyn. Home of the Dodgers, Ebbets Field had a massive scoreboard located in right-centerfield. At the base of the scoreboard, a long, thin billboard, measuring approximately four feet high by 40 feet wide, proclaimed the advantages of shopping at Abe Stark's clothing shop on Pitkin Avenue in the East New York section of Brooklyn. In one corner of the billboard an invitation to batters proclaimed: "HIT SIGN, WIN SUIT!" Stark specialized in GGG suits and gladly would award one to any batter who whacked a ball off the sign. The only problem was that the sign was so situated that it was virtually impossible to hit with a line drive—the sign was too close to the ground. Besides, it was equally difficult to hit with a high fly ball, because they were usually flagged down by either the right or center fielder. The sign later was immortalized in *The New Yorker*

magazine—except in the magazine cartoon the sign was moved to left field and Stark was drawn in, sitting in the front row with a baseball glove in his hand, leaning over to catch the ball before it hit the sign.

Who Was the First Black to Play in the NHL?

Willie O'Ree became the NHL's first black player when he appeared in two games without scoring for the 1957-58 Boston Bruins. The Fredericton, New Brunswick, native earned a second chance in the 1960-61 season after getting off to a hot start with Quebec of the Eastern Professional Hockey League. This time, O'Ree responded by scoring four goals and 10 assists in 43 games. O'Ree's first goal came on New Year's night in Boston. The Bruins were holding a 2-1 lead midway through the third period in a hard-fought contest with the Montreal Canadiens. O'Ree took a pass from Leo Boivin and faked his way past Jean-Guy Talbot and Tom Johnson. Now Willie found himself in front of Canadien goalie Charlie Hodge, whom he had played against in the Eastern Professional League. "I always used to shoot high on him because he's such a little guy," O'Ree recalled. However, before the game, Bruin scoring ace Bronco Horvath advised Willie to keep his shots low. "When I got past Johnson that thing about shooting low flashed into my mind. I shot low, and I sure was happy to see that red light go on!" So were the Boston fans, who responded by giving O'Ree a two-minute standing ovation for the NHL's first "soul" goal.

That was O'Ree's final year in the big leagues, but Willie's professional playing days were far from over. O'Ree skated in the minors for the next fourteen seasons, most of them with Los Angeles and San Diego of the Western Hockey League, where he was one of the league's most popular players because of his great skating ability. Unfortunately, Willie's shooting and stickhandling skills were less than spectacular, and he never played in the NHL again.

Who Was the Only Horse to Ever Defeat Man O' War?

A horse appropriately named Upset defeated Man O' War in the Sanford Stakes at Saratoga Park in 1919. Man O' War had already established himself as two-year-old champion, and as one of the great juveniles of all time, having won six of six starts, including five stakes. Off these impressive credentials, Man O' War was established as the prohibitive 1-2 betting choice. The Sanford figured to be a two-horse race, but the second horse was not Upset, but rather a respected colt named Golden Broom. This was the latter's first crack at Man O' War, and he was sent postward at odds of 2-1. Upset was offered at 7-1, with the other four entries being big longshots.

Man O' War was known for his great starts, but that was not the case in the Sanford. Upset and Golden Broom broke on top, with Man O' War breaking second to last. Golden Broom set the pace, with Upset right behind. Meanwhile, Man O' War was closing the gap, but at the top of the stretch, the champion ran into some traffic problems before moving clear on the outside. Upset moved to challenge Golden Broom, who gave up the lead. Man O' War closed the gap on Upset, but ran out of track. Upset held on to win by a neck.

Man O' War never lost again in three more stakes as a two-year-old, and eleven starts, all stakes, as a three-year-old. His triumphs included a twenty-length win in the Belmont Stakes, and an incredible one-hundred-length victory in the Lawrence Realization Stakes, also at Belmont. Three times in his career Man O' War went off at odds of 1 to 100. His only upset was to Upset.

What Golfer Credited His PGA Tournament Victory to the Use of a Five-Dollar Putter?

In 1964 golfer Bobby Nichols won the PGA tournament at the Columbus Country Club, in Columbus, Ohio, using a five-dollar putter he had bought in a local pro shop in his hometown, Louisville, Kentucky.

The story goes that while Nichols was attending a party at the Owl Creek Country Club in Louisville, he got feeling restless in anticipation of his upcoming PGA tournament, so he wandered off for a walk. He wound up in the pro shop toying with various sale items. While he was there he came across a used putter that just felt right in his hands. Inquiring about the price, which was five dollars, Nichols bought it immediately.

His new five-dollar putter had a dynamic effect on Nichols' game in the tournament. He shot a first-round 64 while carding eight birdies and sinking four putts of more than ten feet.

By the third round Nichols was still going strong and only his putter saved him from a disastrous round. Scoring a 69 in the face of disaster, Nichols holed putts from ten, fifteen, twenty, and twenty-five feet out.

As the fourth round of play began Nichols and his lucky putter were still going strong. On the tenth hole Nichols knocked in a beautiful 35-foot putt for an eagle. He made putts of 15 and 10 feet on the fifteenth and sixteenth holes, respectively, but the best was yet to come. On the seventeenth hole Nichols was standing over a 50 foot putt. But like he had done all tournament long he rolled the ball right into the cup.

Bobby Nichols' unbelievable four days of putting had made him PGA champ. What was more astounding than Nichols winning was the way he went about his victory. He made only 119 putts over the course of 72 holes. Even Jack Nicklaus had made 134 putts for the tournament. But Bobby Nichols knew why. He gave full credit to the five-dollar putter he picked up in a local pro-shop.

Which Red Sox Player Was Involved in Two Brawls with the New York Yankees?

Carlton Fisk faced off against the Bronx Bombers in a "preliminary" bout in 1973, and helped ignite the "main event" in 1976.

Home plate at Fenway was transformed into a war zone in 1973, all because Gene Michael of the Yankees missed a suicide squeeze bunt. The runner from third, Thurman Munson, noticed Fisk, Boston's pride of home plate, catch the ball and brace himself for a collision between the two best young catchers in the American League. Munson was ready, too—with elbows way up. *BANG!* Fisk absorbed the full impact of Munson's 188 pounds, landed on his American Express card and came up swinging. Both Munson and Michael then attacked Fisk, leaving him with a bruised eye and a scratched face.

"The Yankees and Red Sox have played this way since baseball was invented," says Fisk. "I must admit we get out there against them with a lot of intensity. Sometimes we get carried away a little."

In 1976, on a warm Thursday night in May, Boston's flaky lefthanded pitcher Bill Lee almost had to be carried away himself, following a bench-clearing brawl with the hated New Yorkers in the refurbished Yankee Stadium. The defending American League champs trailed the first-place Yankees by six games as the two clubs began a four-game weekend series.

In the bottom half of the sixth inning, New York was threatening to add to their precarious 1-0 lead with Lou Piniella on second base and Graig Nettles on first. The batter, Otto Velez, lined a Lee fastball into right field. The Sox' Dwight Evans, who earlier had thrown out Yankee Fred Stanley at home plate, again was challenged to retire a base runner.

As Piniella chugged around third base with the green light from coach Dick Howser, the charging Evans scooped up the ball, reared back, and fired an accurate one-hop throw to catcher Fisk.

The Sox' talented backstop received the skidding throw on the first-base side of the plate, turned on his knees to meet the sliding Yankee runner and tagged him out. But it didn't end there.

Piniella thought the ball had been jarred loose by the collision and tried desperately to kick it away so that umpire Terry Cooney would see it. Instead of the ball, Piniella inadvertently kicked Fisk.

"I was down on my knees with the ball," Fisk said, "and the next thing I know, his knees are at my head. We went down and he's rolling and kicking all over the place. It was his kicking that started the whole thing. He was being malicious."

Having suffered several painful groin injuries on previous plays like this one, Fisk took exception to Piniella's actions. He tagged him with the ball a second time—only harder—in the jaw. Lou grabbed the catcher's chest protector to get out from under him and Fisk rapped him again on the chin, this time with the ball in his bare right hand. Then the donnybrook began.

At that moment, Boston first baseman Carl Yastrzemski and Yankee on-deck hitter Sandy Alomar raced to home plate to act as peacemakers. The rest of the players figured Yastrzemski and Alomar were going to fight, too, so they stormed to the diamond with fists cocked.

Bill Lee was the next "outsider" to join the fracas, followed by the Yankees' Velez and Nettles, who put both his arms around the Boston pitcher, to try and drag him off the pile-up of players.

"I heard him (Lee) yelling that his shoulder was hurt," Nettles recalled. "If I wanted to punch him right there I could have killed him, but I didn't. At that point I just wanted to break it up."

Meanwhile, New York outfielder Mickey Rivers, who also had charged out of the dugout to lend physical support, jumped Lee from behind, dragged him to the ground with a hammerlock and uncorked a number of vicious hammerlike punches in a windmill manner.

With Boston's ace lefthander now lying on the ground in pain, Nettles tried to explain to a few of Lee's teammates that he only wanted to get him off the pile. Suddenly, Lee got up, walked over to Nettles and delivered a barrage of invectives that made the Yankee third baseman sorry he even attempted to make peace. At one point, Lee told Nettles, "If you ever hurt my shoulder again, I'll kill you." That was all the usually mild-mannered Nettles had to hear.

"He started screaming at me like he was crazy," Graig said. "There were tears in his eyes. He told me he was going to get me, and that's when he started coming after me. I wasn't going to back off anymore."

Nettles then connected with a right cross to the eye which decked Lee. They finished their private war on the ground. By now the pain in Lee's shoulder was excruciating. Red Sox' trainer Charley Moss rushed to the aid of the fallen pitcher and escorted him to the dressing room. It turned out to be Lee's last appearance in uniform for about six weeks.

The rest of the casualty list read like a typical weekly National Football League injury report. Carl Yastrzemski suffered a bruised thigh, Mickey Rivers injured his foot, Lou Piniella hurt his hand but, miraculously, the injury-prone Carlton Fisk escaped unscathed.

"It was the worst fight I've ever seen," Yankee first base coach Elston Howard commented after the fist-swinging subsided.

What Boston Celtic Great Came to Beantown by Virtue of Being Picked Out of a Hat?

Bob Cousy. Having completed an illustrious college career at Holy Cross University in Worcester, Massachusetts, Bob Cousy was a New England celebrity. Cousy wanted nothing more than to play professional basketball with the Boston Celtics, just a short trip down the road from Worcester.

But the Celtics disappointed Cousy, as well as their fans, by selecting Charley Share of Bowling Green. Coach Red

Auerbach responded to the public outcry by saying, "Am I supposed to win, or am I supposed to worry about the local yokels?" Meanwhile, Cousy was selected by the Tri-Cities, a franchise representing the booming towns of Rock Island and Moline, Illinois, and Davenport, Iowa. After signing a distraught Cousy, the Tri-Cities promptly traded him to the Chicago Stags. But the Stags folded before the season, allowing its players to sign with other teams.

A conflict arose between the Celtics, the New York Knicks, and the Philadelphia Warriors. There were three ex-Stags remaining: veterans Andy Phillips and Max Zaslofsky, and Cousy. All three teams wanted Zaslofsky. NBA President Maurice Podoloff ruled that the names of each player would be placed in a hat, and the three teams would draw a player. The Celtics picked first—and got "stuck" with Bob Cousy.

If Red Auerbach was upset, he wasn't mad very long. Cousy won the rookie of the year award in 1950-51, in the first of his brilliant thirteen years with the Celtics.

Who Was the Biggest Little Star of the New York Football Yankees?

Claude "Buddy" Young. 5-4½, 164 pounds. A little black halfback who had starred at the University of Illinois, Young turned pro with the New York Yankees of the All-America Football Conference in 1947 and played with them until the young league was absorbed by the National Football League, following the 1949 season. He remained with the NFL Yanks and became a tremendous crowd-pleaser. "I've never seen an athlete arouse a crowd the way Buddy Young can," Pittsburgh Steelers' owner Art Rooney said.

In 1952 the Yankees were shifted to Dallas and then to Baltimore where, in 1954, Young was voted the Colts' most popular player. He retired prior to the 1956 season.

Which Rodeo Bucking Bronco Had a Monument Erected in His Honor?

Midnight, who died in 1936, had a monument built in his memory at Plattsville, Colorado. The horse was best known for being the only one that the accomplished saddle bronc rider Pete Knight could not ride. Knight launched his career bucking broncs at the age of 15, and won his first rodeo event five years later. In time, Knight had taken on, and defeated, every horse on the rodeo circuit, except Midnight. Rodeo fans were anticipating the classic confrontation with great glee, but Knight's fans were disappointed each of the three times the champion rider attempted to hang on to the vigorous 1,200-pound animal. In 1932, at Cheyenne, Kansas, Knight made his most valiant attempt, staying on Midnight's back for seven of the required ten seconds. But the horse prevailed and proved himself unbeatable.

Midnight was forced into retirement in 1935 because of injured legs and finally died in 1936. Rodeo riders mourned his passing, and the monument in Colorado was erected with the following poem inscribed:

Underneath this sod lies a great bucking horse,
There never lived a cowboy he couldn't toss.
His name was Midnight, his coat black as coal,
If there's a hoss heaven, please God, rest his soul.

Which Tennis Star Refused to Take the Court at Wimbledon Upon Hearing that Queen Mary Was in the Audience?

According to Wimbledon historian Al Laney, who for years was tennis expert for the *New York Herald-Tribune*, there have been only two incidents at Wimbledon in connection with royalty when the tradition and routine were broken. The first occurred in 1926, the year of Wimbledon's jubilee celebration. At the time the reigning queen of the center court was the French ace, Suzanne Lenglen.

Because of Mademoiselle Lenglen's artistry and because of Wimbledon's anniversary, Queen Mary of England made a special pilgrimage to the tennis courts, primarily to see Mlle. Lenglen perform. However, the temperamental Frenchwoman refused to go on the court.

Although she was considered the belle of tennis, Suzanne had pressed her luck too far. A day later she *did* appear, only to resounding boos from the audience. It was the only instance in all of Wimbledon's history that a star was booed upon taking the court. Mlle. Lenglen never played another match at Wimbledon.

The second breach of etiquette at Wimbledon was less traumatic. In the 1935 semifinal round young Don Budge of the United States was playing the aristocratic Baron Gottfried von Cramm. During the second set Queen Mary made her entrance. The Baron bowed but the naive Budge was unschooled in the etiquette of Wimbledon and walked in circles as the Queen took her seat.

The players changed courts at the end of their game, and now it was Budge's turn to officially pay homage to the Queen but, unfortunately, he didn't know the proper method. Instead of standing at attention and then bowing, Budge casually grinned and waved his hand at Queen Mary. Although she was startled and properly perturbed at first, Her Majesty also smiled, half-waved, and then bowed. The crowd cheered "God Bless The Queen" and cheered Budge as well.

"Two years later," wrote Laney, "when Budge had become champion by beating Cramm in the final, Queen Mary received them in the royal box. Budge knew what to do by now. He was as correct as the baron himself. But he still grinned at the Queen and the Queen grinned back."

What Runner Introduced the Idea of Pacing Oneself in Long-Distance Events?

Paavo Nurmi of Finland. Before Nurmi, runners competed solely against each other in long-distance races, with no regard to how fast they were going in the early stages. When Great Britain's Walter George broke the mile record, going the distance in 4:18.4 in 1884, George ran all out in the early going, and staggered across the finish line. Many distance races were run in this manner. But Paavo Nurmi, who set 22 world records from 1920 to 1931, changed the whole concept of the distance event.

Nurmi trained for competition by running behind a trolley. He was the first runner to ever run with a stopwatch in his hand, carefully calculating how fast to go so that he would have enough left to defeat his rivals. Going into the last lap, Nurmi tossed the stopwatch to the ground and turned on the speed.

In the 1924 Olympics, Nurmi, in a three-day span, won the preliminaries and the finals for both the 1,500 and 5,000 meters, with the 5,000 meter final coming minutes after the completion of the 1,500 meter event. The next day, Nurmi contributed to the Finnish team's victory in the 3,000 meter relay heats. The following day, he won the gold medal in the 10,000 meter cross-country race in one hundred degree heat. Finally, Paavo Nurmi completed an amazing six days of competition by helping the Finnish team win the finals of the 3,000 meter relay. One would have to say that Paavo Nurmi did a pretty good job of pacing himself in the 1924 Olympics.

Who Hit the Only Fair Ball Out of Yankee Stadium?

Josh Gibson, Pittsburgh Crawfords, 1934. The legendary black catcher— many consider him the most proficient of all time and a better slugger than Babe Ruth—Gibson hit his home run in a Negro National League game against the Philadelphia Stars. One witness was Jack Marshall of the Chicago American Giants who recalled: "Josh hit the ball over the triple deck next to the bullpen in left field. Over and out! I never will forget that, because we were getting ready to leave because we were going to play a night game and we were standing in the aisle when that boy hit this ball!''

Baseball's bible, the *Sporting News,* credits Gibson with hitting a longer home run than Ruth ever hit in Yankee Stadium, a drive that hit just two feet from the top of the Stadium wall circling the bleachers in centerfield, about 580 feet from home plate. It was estimated that had the blast been two feet higher it would have cleared the wall and traveled about 700 feet.

Walter Johnson, one of the best pitchers of all time, watched Gibson in action and observed: "There is a catcher that any big-league club would like to buy for $200,000. His name is Gibson . . . he can do everything. He hits the ball a mile. And he catches so easy, he might as well be in a rocking chair. Throws like a rifle. Bill Dickey (the Yankee great) isn't as good a catcher. Too bad this Gibson is a colored fellow.''

One legend has it that Gibson was playing at Forbes Field in Pittsburgh one day and hit such a towering drive that nobody saw it come down. After long deliberation, the umpire ruled it a home run. A day later Gibson's team was playing in Philadelphia when suddenly a ball dropped out of the sky and was caught by an alert centerfielder on the opposition. Pointing to Gibson, the umpire ruled: "You're out—yesterday in Pittsburgh!''

Which Professional Football Team Perfected the T-Formation?

The Chicago Bears, 1940. Coached by George Halas, the Bears of the National Football League merely improved upon a play that had been part of the woof and warp of the gridiron since the turn of the century. But for reasons best known to the professional coaches only such plays as the single wing, double wing, and old Notre Dame shift had become standards. George Halas saw better possibilities with the

T-formation. He set the Bears' quarterback directly behind the center. Behind the quarterback was the fullback, along with two halfbacks parallel to the line of scrimmage. As the 1940 season unfolded—during which Chicago lost only three games—Halas employed the T-formation more often, especially when he realized that opponents could not adequately defend against the creative assault.

By far the most persuasive case for the T-formation was made on December 8, 1940, when Washington and the Bears clashed for the NFL championship. Led by ace passer Sammy Baugh, the Redskins had already beaten Chicago 7-3, three weeks earlier and were considered a fair bet to do it again for the title. But on the second play of the game the Bears' T-formation produced a touchdown and, by halftime, the score was 28-0. The game became so lopsided in Chicago's favor that by the fourth quarter the referee pleaded with Halas to limit his plays so that the footballs used for extra points would not be kicked into the stands (where fans could keep the pigskin). Unfortunately there was only one football left. Halas agreed and the Bears won the game, 73-0, one of the worst routs in NFL history. Within a year nearly every major football team had incorporated the T-formation into its repertoire.

Which Was the First American Football League Team to Win the Super Bowl?

The New York Jets, 1969. In Super Bowl III, the Jets were pitted against the National Football League champion Baltimore Colts. In the first two Super Bowl events the NFL's Green Bay Packers easily romped over the AFL champions. There was no reason to believe that the Jets would win the title in 1969, and powerful Baltimore entered the game as a 17-point favorite.

At least one personality thought the odds were ridiculous—Jets' quarterback Joe Namath. A onetime star with Bear Bryant's University of Alabama Crimson Tide, Namath had become known as Broadway Joe. He was cool and confident and talked up a Jets' victory throughout the week preceding the big game. Once, he encountered Colts' place-kicker Lou Michaels in a restaurant and taunted his foe to such an intense degree that the two nearly came to blows.

When they met again on the Orange Bowl turf, the Colts appeared like the underdogs and not the Jets. New York led 7-0 at halftime, added a field goal in the third quarter, then another field goal, and still another. Trailing 0-16, the Colts had become desperate as time ticked away. Baltimore's wily veteran Johnny Unitas began turning the tide, but the best the Colts could do was come up with one touchdown before the gun sounded and New York walked off with the championship.

Whose Death Attracted the Largest Crowd Ever to Attend a Funeral for a Professional Athlete?

Oscar Bonavena, May 1976, Buenos Aires, Argentina. Shot to death in a bizarre episode outside a brothel in Mustang, Nevada, Bonavena was mourned throughout his native land. Eventually, the boxer's body was shipped home to Buenos Aires where 25,000 people waited at the airport or along the road into town. The next day, 150,000 people came to Luna Park, where the Argentine heavyweight champion lay in state all day. According to officials, the city had not seen so many mourners since Carlos Gardel, the famous tango singer, died in 1935.

How Did the Stanley Cup Get Its Name?

The Stanley Cup was named after Lord Stanley of Preston, the governor general of Canada, in 1893. Since the Stanley Cup is a pretty important trophy in the hockey world, one would think that Lord Stanley was an important hockey person. However, not only was Lord Stanley not a hockey person, but he had absolutely nothing to do with the sport.

It was Lord Stanley's son, Arthur Stanley, who was the hockey fan in the family, and Arthur convinced his dad to purchase the trophy and present it to the nation's top amateur team. Thus the Stanley Cup was born, and it was competed for by amateurs from 1893 until the professional Quebec Bulldogs won it in 1912.

What NHL Team Won and Lost the Stanley Cup on the Same Day?

The 1924 Montreal Canadiens. The Canadiens had defeated Ottawa, Vancouver, and Calgary in the playoffs to capture the ice title and, as a tribute to the winners, the citizens of Montreal hailed the Cup kings with a public reception.

The Cup officially was presented to the Canadiens and all players received mementoes from the University of Montreal. (It was the only time in history that a professional hockey club had been so honored by a major learning institution.)

Following the reception, the Canadiens repaired to the home of club owner Leo Dandurand for an informal get-together. Goalie Georges Vezina, Sprague Cleghorn, Sylvio Mantha, and Dandurand climbed into a Model-T Ford to make the trip.

Climbing the Cote St. Antoine Road hill in Westmount, the Ford stalled and all the occupants, but the driver, climbed out to give it a push.

That's when the Cup-winners became the Cup-losers. Dandurand recalled the episode as follows:

"Cleghorn, who had been jealously carrying the hard-won Stanley Cup in his lap, deposited it on the curb at the roadside before he joined us in shoving the car up the hill. When we reached the top, we hopped back into the car and resumed our hockey chatter as we got going again.

"Upon reaching my house, we all started in on a big bowl of punch which my wife had prepared. It wasn't until she asked, 'Well, where IS this Stanley Cup you've been talking about?' that we realized that Cleghorn had left it on the side of the road.

"Sprague and I drove hurriedly back to the spot almost an hour after we had pushed the car up the hill. There was the Cup in all its shining majesty, still sitting on the curb of the busy street!"

Who Was the Only Tennis Player to Consistently Beat Bill Tilden?

Tilden defeated every player more times than he lost—except for Ellsworth Vines. Vines, said by many to possess the greatest serve the game has ever known, won 61 of 80 matches against Tilden.

"During his pro career," Brave Dyer of the *Los Angeles Times* said, "which ran from 1934 through 1939, H. Ellsworth Vines, Jr., won 257 and lost 130 matches.

"The only player to win a majority of matches from him was J. Donald Budge, who won 22 of 39 played in 1939. Vines won 61 and lost 19 with Tilden; against Hans Nusslein he won 28 and lost 11; against Lester Stoefen, he won 27 and lost 4; won all 10 against Henri Cochet; against Martin Plaa, won 8 and lost 2; against Robert Ramilion, won 6 and lost 1.

"Vines and (Frederick J.) Perry played 157 matches of which Vines won 86 and lost 71."

Which High-Risk Sport Originally Called for Compulsory Participation by Women Alongside Men?

Bobsledding. An outgrowth of tobogganing, bobsledding was developed in Switzerland late in the 19th century

when toboggans were mounted on sledlike runners. The sleds were extremely fast and excessively dangerous, so in 1895 a much heavier sled, called "Bobsleigh," was invented.

The St. Moritz Bobsleigh Club mapped a course down the Swiss Alps using sleds that carried five passengers. Rules stipulated that two passengers be women. But because the sport was so intrinsically dangerous, few women were willing to participate. Hence, the rules were amended to allow stout men to substitute for the women. However, in the first race at Cresta Run at the initial organized Bobsleigh Festival on January 5, 1898, two of the five passengers were, in fact, women.

What Was the First Major League Franchise Shift in Half a Century?

Boston Braves to Milwaukee, National League. Once a baseball institution, the Braves vacated Boston for Milwaukee in time for the 1953 season. Although few baseball barons would admit it at the time, the switch served as a catalyst for many more franchise moves. In 1954, the St. Louis Browns moved to Baltimore and became the Orioles. Following the 1957 season the Brooklyn Dodgers and New York Giants moved from New York City to become the Los Angeles Dodgers and San Francisco Giants, respectively.

The Braves turned out to be the prime carpetbaggers. After a relatively short stay in Milwaukee, the erstwhile Boston nine moved, in 1965, to Atlanta.

The spate of transfers eventually inspired lawsuits. In 1969 the City of Seattle filed a $11,000,000 suit against the American League and its 12 clubs after the league decided to move the expansion Seattle Pilots to Milwaukee and change the club's name to the Brewers.

Who Was the Last of the Legal Spitball Pitchers?

Burleigh Grimes. Although the spitball—doctoring the baseball with saliva, tobacco juice, or sandpaper—was outlawed in 1919, eighteen spitball practitioners were permitted to continue throwing "wet ones" until the end of their careers. The mean, outspoken, and fearless Grimes lasted the longest, racking up 218 victories in 18 seasons, with the Brooklyn Dodgers, Pittsburgh Pirates, and three other teams before retiring in 1934.

They called Grimes "Ole Stubblebeard" and he was revered as one of the most colorful characters of baseball's Golden Age. A hot-tempered Wisconsin farm boy, he became a big winner after mastering the art of the spitball. After his retirement as an active major leaguer, Grimes turned to managing and always insisted that baseball never should have outlawed the spitball. In fact, he campaigned for its legalization as "a perfectly safe pitch . . . easier to control than the knuckleball."

He was voted into the Hall of Fame in 1964, and when he surpassed his 80th birthday Grimes told an interviewer that he was as fearless as ever. "I just got married again!" he laughed.

Who Was the Pitcher Off Whom Babe Ruth Hit His "Called-Shot" Home Run?

Charley Root. The 1932 World Series between the New York Yankees and Chicago Cubs was one of the most bitterly played between the National and American League representatives. The Yankees won the first two games, 12-6 and 5-2, at Yankee Stadium, but the third and fourth games were scheduled for hostile Wrigley Field in Chicago.

Cubs fans not only resented the pompous Yankees, led by the 37-year-old Ruth and his home-run hitting sidekick Lou Gehrig, but they were angry that their team had dropped two games in a row. Prior to the game Ruth and Gehrig further enraged the crowd by hitting a total of 18 "home runs" into the bleachers during batting practice.

Ruth replied by hitting a legitimate home run in his first at bat against pitcher Charley Root in the first inning. But the Cubs rallied and when Ruth came to bat in the fifth inning the score was tied, 3-3. As Ruth glanced at the mound, fans taunted him with chants of "big belly," and "baboon." Root followed with a called strike, whereupon Ruth raised a finger indicating the count. The second pitch was a ball, so Ruth raised a finger on each hand. He did likewise until the count reached two and two.

At this juncture, Ruth lifted his arm and pointed to center-field, clearly indicating to most onlookers that he was planning to plant the next pitch over the fence for another home run. The already angry crowd became even surlier until Root delivered the pitch and Ruth drove the ball precisely where he had predicted it would go.

Instead of bombarding the Babe with more insults the stunned crowd suddenly began applauding the man they had come to hate. Perhaps they realized that Ruth was in the twilight of his great career and that they never would see such a feat again. Whatever the case, New York swept the series in four straight games, for Ruth's last appearance in a World Series. He retired two years later, claiming that his "called shot" was his "dumbest" move. "If I'd missed," Ruth explained, "I'd have looked like an awful fool."

Name the Popular Story-Telling Comedian Who Doubled as a Baseball and Hockey Announcer?

Ward Wilson. A veteran of show business and narrator of the film classic, *The Golden Age of Comedy,* Wilson frequently appeared on radio as host of the show, "Can You Top This?" One of Wilson's gags about an elephant whose trunk was bitten by a crocodile obtained one of the longest laughs in radio history. Wilson also was play-by-play and color commentator for New York Ranger broadcasts and sports analyst on a pre-game Brooklyn Dodgers radio program called "Wilson, Glickman, and Lee." The Glickman was Marty Glickman and the Lee was Bert Lee, Sr.

Which Female Tennis Star Was Also Famous for Lace Panties and Outspoken Broadcasting?

Gussie Moran. A rising star in 1945, the attractive Miss Moran grew more and more popular—and more accomplished—in the post World War II years. Inspired by British designer Teddy Tinling, Gussie wore lace panties at Wimbledon and created a sensation in the sports world. She was, according to one observer, to tennis what Marilyn Monroe was to the movies.

Ironically, Miss Moran was considered a shy person by close friends, but she obviously enjoyed the attention she was receiving and continued to exploit the lace panties routine. In Egypt she made headlines, playing a final match in black shorts. But Gussie was more concerned with tennis than her good looks and soon traded in her panties for more conventional attire. She didn't, however, avoid controversy. She signed on as a baseball commentator for Brooklyn Dodgers' pre-game and post-game broadcasts, and established a reputation as an insightful and outspoken critic.

Which Obscure College Was Responsible for the Biggest Upset in Harvard's Football History?

Centre College, Danville, Kentucky, October 30, 1921. More than 43,000 fans at the Cambridge, Mass. stadium witnessed the upset as Bo McMillan quarterbacked Centre to a 6-0 conquest of mighty Harvard. Until that fateful afternoon, Harvard had won or tied 25 games in a row, including a win over Oregon in the Rose Bowl.

The triumph, however, had been well-planned. The architect was Robert L. "Chief" Myers, who did the recruiting for Centre as head coach. Myers took over in 1917 and slowly but relentlessly built a powerhouse. In 1916 Centre lost to Kentucky, 68-0, but the following year, Centre edged Kentucky, 3-0.

In 1919, Centre beat a strong West Virginia team, one which had earlier beaten Princeton. Word of Centre's ascendency began to get around and Eddie Mahan, scouting for Harvard, suggested that the Crimson add Centre to its schedule. Harvard accepted the advice and, in 1920, Harvard played Centre and won easily, 31-14. At the conclusion of the game Harvard's captain Arnold Horween offered the game ball to Captain McMillan of Centre, but the losing captain refused the offer. "We'll be back next year," said McMillan, "to take it home with us."

McMillan was right. With the score tied, 0-0, in their 1921 rematch, McMillan launched the decisive march at the start of the third quarter. With the ball on Harvard's 32, McMillan went all the way for the one and only touchdown of the fray. The win was so wildly hailed in Danville, Kentucky, that business closed down for a week.

What Kentucky Derby Winner Was "Touted" to a National Magazine Before It Was Born?

Iron Liege, the winner of the 1957 Kentucky Derby. In the fall of 1953, *Sports Illustrated* asked father and son trainers B.A. and Jimmy Jones of the powerful Calumet Farm stable to pick out one of the stable's brood mares as the one they thought was most likely to produce a top racehorse. The magazine's idea was to follow the designated mare's foal throughout his career, starting with the day of his birth. The Joneses selected Iron Maiden, and *Sports Illustrated* was on hand in April of 1954, when Iron Maiden gave birth to a colt to be named Iron Liege. Little did anyone know that out of about 17,000 registered foals in 1954, the Joneses had miraculously selected the one that would go on to win the 1957 Kentucky Derby.

Actually, in the weeks leading up to the '57 Derby, the Joneses' main hope for the Roses was not Iron Liege, but a colt named General Duke, who was coming off a world record performance in the Florida Derby, one of the top Kentucky Derby preps. But General Duke developed an ankle problem and, despite all-out efforts to get him sound for the Derby, had to be scratched on the morning of the race. So Calumet sent out Iron Liege, but the colt was not given much of a chance by anyone. The field for the Derby included such standouts as Bold Ruler, Gallant Man, and Round Table. Thus Iron Liege was sent postward as the 8-1 fourth choice.

The early pacesetter was a sprinter named Federal Hill, who won the Derby Trial on the Tuesday before Derby Day. Iron Liege, with jockey Bill Hartack, was third behind Bold Ruler, with Gallant Man positioned a distant seventh by Willie Shoemaker. Down the backstretch, Bold Ruler moved up to challenge, despite attempts by jockey Eddie Arcaro to restrain him; so Hartack had Iron Liege in perfect position behind the two dueling leaders. As they rounded the final turn, Iron Liege moved up along the rail and took the lead from the tiring pacesetters. As they came down the stretch, Shoemaker moved Gallant Man into contention on the outside. As they approached the sixteenth pole, they were noses apart—Iron Liege on the rail, and Gallant Man closing in on the outside. But suddenly, Shoemaker, misjudging the finish line, raised up in the saddle for a split second. The Shoe recovered and resumed his drive, but Iron Liege held on to win by a nose. "Everyone says I blew it by standing up before the finish line," Shoemaker recalled. "Well, I think I blew it."

For Bill Hartack, the victory was his first of five Derby wins. Round Table rallied for third, and Bold Ruler tired to fourth, completing the greatest top four finishers in Kentucky Derby history. The quartet went on to compile a combined 91 wins and almost $3.5 million in winnings; the four's offspring accounted for more than 180 stakes victories, and almost $39 million in purse money.

Under incredible circumstances, Iron Liege's story in *Sports Illustrated* was completed with a legendary Kentucky Derby victory.

Who Set or Equaled Four World Track Records in 45 Minutes?

Jesse Owens, May 25, 1935. Owens was competing for the Ohio State Buckeyes in the Big Ten Conference Championships. At 3:15 P.M. Owens ran the 100-yard dash in 9.4 seconds, tying the world record. Ten minutes later, Owens competed in the long jump, and leaped 26 feet, 8¼ inches, shattering the world standard by six inches. Just nine minutes later, at 3:34, Owens completed the 220-yard low hurdles in 22.6 seconds, breaking a world record that had been on the books for eleven years. Then, at 4:00, Owens completed his feat by running the 220-yard dash in 20.3 seconds, erasing the world mark of 20.6. Owens' 220 hurdles record was not broken until 1966, and the 220 dash and long jump records stood until 1960.

Owens went on to the Olympics the following year in Berlin and took the gold in the 100 and 200 meter runs, as well as the broad jump, setting records in each.

Who Is the Only Man Ever to Repeat as Olympic Decathlon Gold Medalist?

Bob Mathias of the United States, 1948 and 1952. Perhaps even more incredible than the fact that Mathias won the decathlon twice are the circumstances under which he won his first in 1948. The Californian was only seventeen years old when he won his first gold. Only three months before the Games, Mathias had *never competed* in half of the events required for the decathlon. He had never pole-vaulted, never had competed in the broad jump or javelin, and had never run in the 400 and 1500 meter runs. When his high school coach suggested that he tryout for the U.S. Olympic team decathlon squad, Mathias had only three weeks to practice his new events before the regional Olympic trials. Despite his inexperience, Mathias advanced to the finals of the trials, and won the U.S. decathlon championship, clinching a spot on the Olympic team.

At the end of the first day of the Olympic decathlon in London, Mathias was third of the 28 participants, with his best finish being a tie for first in the high jump, one of the events that he was more experienced in. The following day, Mathias faced three events that he had just started three months earlier—the pole vault, the javelin throw, and the grueling final event, the 1,500 meter run. To make matters worse, the weather was typical London—rain and fog. The fog was so dense that the officials had to shine flashlights on the javelin take-off line. Despite a slippery pole, Mathias gained a first-place tie on the pole vault. It was on this day Mathias won the discus event, the only competition that he won outright. By the time Mathias was preparing for the 1,500 meter run, he had built an insurmountable lead. All he had to do was to finish the 1,500 in decent time; instead, he won the event in 5 minutes and 11 seconds. His final point total was 7,139; no one else reached 7,000.

Thus it is no surprise that four years later, at the age of 21 and with four years and three months of practice, Bob Mathias repeated as Olympic decathlon winner in Helsinki.

Who Was the First NBA Player to Break His Own One-Game Scoring Record?

Elgin Baylor. As a member of the Minneapolis Lakers, Baylor scored 64 points against the Boston Celtics on November 8, 1959, at Minnesota. A year later, on November 15, 1960, as a member of the Los Angeles Lakers, Baylor scored 71 points against the New York Knicks at Madison Square Garden. Baylor's record lasted until December 8,

1961, when Wilt Chamberlain of the Philadelphia Warriors scored 78 points against Los Angeles. Chamberlain then broke his own mark—and became the first to reach the 100-point plateau—when he scored 100 points for Philadelphia against New York on March 2, 1962.

Which Was the First Canadian Franchise in the National Basketball Association?

The Toronto Huskies, 1946. Professional basketball was less than a hit at Maple Leaf Gardens, but the Huskies were notable for their high-scoring star Ed Sadowski. In the 1946-47 season he twice set individual one-game scoring records. On November 1, 1946, playing against the New York Knickerbockers at Maple Leaf Gardens, Sadowski scored 18 points. The mark was twice broken—first by Frank Baumholtz (25) and then Max Zaslofsky (28)—before Sadowski set a new record of 30 on November 15, 1946 against Providence at Toronto. Unfortunately, Sadowski could not single-handedly convert Toronto into a basketball town, and the team soon gave way to the more popular Toronto Maple Leafs hockey team.

What Beer Had Its Jingle Played at Madison Square Garden After Ranger Goals?

Eichler beer sponsored New York Ranger broadcasts back in the 1940s. Eichler's theme was "You're the Tops" as in the Cole Porter song, and the jingle helped make the beer a popular one in New York. The Ranger radio broadcast team of Bert Lee, Sr., and Ward Wilson came up with a scheme to help sell the beer. Their brainstorm was called the "Eichler Automatic Goal Judge," although it was not as its name described. The device was simply a series of three horns that beeped the tune for "You're the Tops." Following a Ranger

score, Lee shouted, "And now for the Eichler Automatic
Goal Judge," and Garden fans would be treated to the Eichler jingle, which, hopefully for the Eichler company, would
remind the Ranger fans of their favorite brew. It was a cute
idea, but any positive effects it might have had on Eichler
beer sales soon wore off, as Schaefer beer became the
Ranger sponsor and Eichler faded into extinction. Lee
wanted to build a Schaefer Automatic Goal Judge, but it
would have taken a lot of horns to beep "Our hand has never
lost its skill."

*True or False: Madison Square Garden Once Was Host to a
Football Game.*
   True. And not just one game, but an entire tournament, in
1902. Tournament contestants included teams from Orange,
New Jersey; Watertown, New York; Philadelphia, Pennsylvania; and Franklin, Pennsylvania. The Franklin team won
easily.

Who Telecast the First Super Bowl, in January 1967?
   NBC *and* CBS. It was the first and only time in the history
of the NFL that two networks simultaneously telecast a major
pro football game. The two networks pooled announcers and
technicians to cover the historic first meeting of the NFL and
AFL champions. Since then the networks have rotated
coverage.

What Sport Was Originally a Religious Ceremony?
   Bowling. In ancient Germany, many natives carried a
club, called a "kegel." The kegel was an all-purpose instru-

ment used for twirling (in order to keep one's wrists and
forearms strong), as a hammer, and as a weapon. Few Germans were seen without a kegel. A person implementing his
kegel was called a "kegler," the contemporary German
word for "bowler."

Occasionally Germans were required to demonstrate to
their clerics that they were leading an honorable life. To do so
they were instructed to place their kegel topside on one end of
a long runway, located at the church. The person then was
given a round stone with which to roll at the kegel in the
hopes of knocking it down. If the kegler hit the club, then the
clerics believed that he had led a life of honor. However, if he
missed, he was regarded as a sinner, and required to return in
an effort to improve his aim and morals. The practice was
discontinued in the fifth century.

In time, Germans perceived the sporting value of their
religious ceremony. They would convene, place their kegels
in a group, and take turns rolling stones at them. The one who
knocked over the most kegels was deemed the winner. As
time went on, wooden balls replaced stones, and specially
designed pins replaced kegels.

Pick an All-Star Team of Stars Who Belong in the Hall of Fame But Aren't Members of the Cooperstown Shrine?

First base: Frank Chance is a Hall of Famer, but Johnny
Mize isn't, even though Mize had 2,011 hits and Chance,
1,272. Mize topped Chance in runs, 1,118-797, runs batted
in, 1,337-596, and lifetime batting average, .312-.296.

Second base: Johnny Evers is a member, Red Schoendienst is not, yet Schoendienst had a .289 lifetime batting
average while Evers lifetime average was .270. Schoendienst produced a total of 2,449 hits. Evers' hit total was
1,658.

Shortstop: Bobby Wallace is in, Herman Long is out, yet Long, although he played in nine fewer seasons, had almost as many hits as Wallace and scored 402 more runs. Long played on five pennant winners and was regarded as the finest fielding shortstop at the turn of the century.

Third base: Fred Lindstrom is in, Ed Mathews is out, yet Mathews hit 512 home runs, among the top ten of all time. Mathews scored 1,509 runs to Lindstrom's 895 and drove in 1,453 to Lindstrom's 779.

Left field: Ralph Kiner has been enshrined, Hack Wilson has not, yet Wilson had ten more hits and 47 more runs batted in. Wilson's lifetime average was .307 compared with Kiner's .279.

Centerfield: Max Carey is in, Duke Snider is out, yet Carey was merely a solid hitter while Snider was one of the best belters of all time. In one season or another Snider led the National League in hits, runs, home runs, runs batted in, total bases, and slugging.

Right field: Tommy McCarthy is a member, Chuck Klein is on the outs, yet McCarthy hit for a .292 average while Klein's average lifetime was .320. Besides, Klein led the National League in home runs four times and twice was the runs-batted-in leader. He also led in runs scored three times and in slugging average thrice. For four straight seasons he was a leader in total bases.

Catcher: Roger Bresnahan is in, Ernie Lombardi is out, yet Bresnahan's lifetime average was only .279, while Lombardi had a 17-year average of .306. Bresnahan hit only 27 home runs while Lombardi hit 190. In addition, Lombardi caught 1,542 games, 568 more than Bresnahan.

Pitcher: Jesse Haines is in, Addie Joss is out, yet Joss won 160 games in nine years. Haines pitched for 19 seasons and won a total of 210 games, but in only four seasons did he win more than 13 games. Although a player supposedly should play for ten seasons, Joss' record as well as his earned run average (1.88) should enable him to qualify for induction into the Hall of Fame.

Who Was the First Great "Little" College Football Star?

Walter Eckersall, University of Chicago. Weighing in at 140 pounds. Eckersall was a back in a day when every player played both offense and defense. "Little Eckie," as they called him, could do everything well—run, pass, and kick. He could knock off a 100-yard dash in 9.8 seconds and, although passing still was a rarity in collegiate football, he once connected with a 75-yard pass for a touchdown. It has been said that when it came to field goals, Eckersall was the greatest in the early years of the 20th century. Most amazing of all was his defensive ability and Eckersall's fondness for tackling men almost twice his weight.

One of Eckersall's most noteworthy efforts occurred in 1905 when Chicago took on the University of Michigan Wolverines. At the time Michigan was known as the "point-a-minute" team, having outscored its opponents 495-0 prior to meeting Chicago. But "Little Eckie" and his teammates would not be moved by Michigan, and halfway through the fourth quarter the score was tied at 0-0.

Finally, it appeared that Michigan would break through. The Wolverines carried the ball to Chicago's two-yard-line, where the Maroon held fast and took over. When it appeared that Chicago also was going nowhere, Eckersall executed a brilliant end run, moving the ball to the 50-yard-line. Here, Chicago was stopped, so Eckersall got off a towering kick that was caught by Michigan's Denny Clark in his own end zone. Before Clark could find daylight he was tackled, and Chicago took a 2-0 lead on the safety.

Now Michigan counterattacked and a Wolverine ball carrier bisected the Chicago line and went head-to-head with Eckersall, the safety. "Little Eckie" leaped at his larger foe, but the Michigan player flew over his flying body. Eckersall then did a complete flip-flop with his body and landed on his feet whereupon he dragged down his foe on the Chicago 20-yard-line. The unexpected tackle by Chicago's miniscule wonder took the heart out of the "point-a-minute" team, and Chicago triumphed, 2-0.

How Did a Live Goose Affect the National Hockey League Presidency?

For the most part the presidency of the National Hockey League has been a position surrounded by an aura of dignity. But in the short period between the death of Frank Calder in 1943 and the nomination of Clarence Campbell in 1946, there was a rare lightheartedness combined with the efficiency and dedication usually associated with the office. The cause for the change was the personality of Mervyn "Red" Dutton, who was designated president following the death of Frank Calder.

Unlike Calder and Campbell, Dutton, who played for and subsequently ran the New York Americans, was a rollicking type. His good-natured manner, the cockeyed behavior of the Americans, and the generally nutsy world of hockey in New York in the thirties had inured Red to frolicsome behavior.

The leading characters in what since has become known as "The Case of the Loose Goose" were Dutton, John Digby Chick, vice-president of the American Hockey League, and two Toronto sportswriters, Vern DeGeer and Jim Coleman. Oh, yes, and Mildred the goose.

Dutton, an extrovert given to great bursts of enthusiasm, had reneged on a promise to deliver a dozen ducks to his newspaper admirers after a hunting expedition. The goading of Dutton became intense when the 1943 Stanley Cup semifinals series between the Toronto Maple Leafs and the Detroit Red Wings opened in Detroit on March 21. By the time the series switched to Toronto, the exasperated Dutton had decided to fulfill his promise.

"He smuggled a dead duck into my suitcase," DeGeer recalled. "I knew it was Dutton's work so I decided to get even."

Accompanied by Toronto *Globe and Mail* sportswriter Jim Coleman, DeGeer, the late columnist for the *Montreal Gazette*, went shopping for another duck. "I'm fresh out of well-plucked ducks," explained the poultry man, "but as a special favor I'm going to let you have a goose. This is an exceptional goose, named Mildred, and I do not wish to kill her.''

Aware that Dutton had checked into the Royal York Hotel, the writers decided to sneak Mildred into the president's suite. Having determined that Dutton was not in his room, Coleman persuaded the assistant manager to give him the NHL president's room key. The writers proceeded to Dutton's suite, where they deposited Mildred in the bathtub. DeGeer filled the tub with water, drew the shower curtain, and retreated with Coleman to a hiding place in the room closet.

A few hours later, Dutton returned to freshen himself up for the third playoff game that night. ''I was half-naked when I walked into the bathroom,'' says Dutton. ''As soon as I started shaving, I heard this strange hissing noise from the bathtub. I pulled aside the curtain and this crazy goose flies at me and out of the room.''

Out of the room flew Mildred, then Dutton, then the two howling writers.

Within minutes, DeGeer and Coleman recovered Mildred and this time carried her to the room of the late John Digby Chick, a portly gentleman who had left for the hockey game. Once again, the writers placed Mildred in the bathtub, provided her with water, and drew the curtain.

After the game, Chick indulged in a few drinks and returned to his room. ''He was feeling very little pain,'' says Coleman. ''After getting into his pajamas, he decided to have a nightcap. He poured a short one and went into the bathroom to add some water.''

As he turned on the faucet, Chick felt a pinching sensation on his right thigh. He looked down and observed Mildred leaning out from behind the shower curtain. He stared at her for several seconds, walked back into the bedroom, picked up the telephone and asked for room service. ''Please send the house detective to my room,'' Chick implored. ''There's a goose in my bathtub.''

The call was transferred to the assistant manager, who was

accustomed to dealing with inebriated guests. "Now, Mr. Chick," he said, "you just climb into bed and you'll find the goose is gone when you wake up in the morning."

The assistant manager's prescription failed to calm Chick. "Either get rid of the goose or me," he demanded. "There'd be three house detectives up here if I had a girl in my bathtub."

Flanked by three house detectives, the assistant manager went up to Chick's room and, sure enough, found Mildred phlegmatically floating in the bathtub.

The following day, Mildred was punished for the traumas she had inflicted on the hockey executives. The assistant manager and the house detectives had Mildred for dinner—"but," says Coleman, "not as a guest."

Which Ballplayer Caught in the Opening Game of a Doubleheader and Pitched in the Second Game?

Ted Radcliffe, one of the greatest black baseball players, was the catcher for Satchel Paige in a Negro league doubleheader at Yankee Stadium in 1932 for the famed Pittsburgh Crawfords. The Crawfords won, 5-0. Then Radcliffe took the mound and pitched a 4-0 shutout. As a result, Radcliffe earned the nickname "Double Duty," thanks to journalist Damon Runyon.

After seeing Radcliffe perform, Runyon wrote: "It was worth the admission price of two to see Double Duty out there in action."

Those who played with and against Radcliffe toasted his versatility. "He never got the recognition he should have," said shortstop Jake Stephens. "In my book he was one of the greatest."

Added catcher Royal "Skink" Browning: "Radcliffe could catch the first game, pitch the second—and was a terror at both of them."

Name Ten Hollywood Films About Baseball.

Among the first ever made were two silent films, *How The Office Boy Saw The Ball Game* (1906) and *Bush Leaguer* (1917). Several baseball biographies were made in Hollywood. These include: *Pride Of The Yankees*, starring Gary Cooper as Lou Gehrig; *The Babe Ruth Story*, starring William Bendix; *The Monty Stratton Story*, starring James Stewart; *The Pride Of St. Louis*, starring Dan Dailey as Dizzy Dean; *The Winning Team*, starring Ronald Reagan as Grover Cleveland Alexander; *The Jackie Robinson Story*, starring Jackie Robinson; and *Fear Strikes Out*, starring Anthony Perkins as Jim Piersall.

Among the more notable dramas, there were: *Big Leaguer*, with Edward G. Robinson; *The Kid From Left Field*, with Dan Dailey; and *Bang The Drum Slowly*, with Michael Moriarty and Robert DeNiro.

Musicals abounded, such as: *Take Me Out To The Ball Game*, with Gene Kelly, Frank Sinatra and Esther Williams; and *Damn Yankees*, with Ray Walston, Gwen Verdon and Tab Hunter.

The screen has offered numerous comedies about the national pastime. Some of the best were: *Casey At The Bat*, starring Wallace Beery; *Fast Company*, with Jack Oakie; *Elmer The Great*, with Joe E. Brown; *Alibi Ike*, with Joe E. Brown; *Rhubarb*, with Rhubarb the Cat; *Kill The Umpire*, starring William Bendix; *Angels In The Outfield*, starring Paul Douglas; and *It Happens Every Spring*, with Ray Milland.

What Was the Longest Game in Basketball History?

125 hours between members of the Alpha Sigma fraternity of Rio Grande College, in Rio Grande, Ohio. During the 1973-74 basketball season the members of Alpha Sigma planned a run at the all-time marathon basketball record of

101 hours set by a Massachusetts high school. The only problem was how to organize such an undertaking to insure the availability of enough people to play basketball for more than four straight days.

The organizers decided to go with two 15-man teams. Naturally, each team used only one five-man unit on the court for four hours at a time.

The game began on a Monday and continued through Tuesday, Wednesday, Thursday, and ended on Friday after 125 consecutive hours. The white team was victorious in a 10,752-10,734 contest, after staging a "late" comeback in the game's waning hours.

It is interesting to note that Bevo Francis, the legendary school alumnus, did not participate in the game. Francis, who scored 113, 116, and an all-time record 150 points in single games during his illustrious collegiate career, would have set some new all-time records had he played.

There were no reports about the officiating of the game, although we hope there were ample numbers of officials on hand to share the brunt of their marathon whistle-blowing session.

Who Was the Only Goalie Ever to Score a Goal in Pro Hockey?

No goalie has ever scored a goal in the NHL, but Michel Plasse turned the trick while playing for the St. Louis Blues' Central Hockey League affiliate in Kansas City. Plasse is a journeyman goaltender, having moved from the Blues' organization to the Montreal Canadiens, the Kansas City Scouts, the Pittsburgh Penguins, and back to the Scouts' after they had relocated in Denver.

Plasse's goal came on the night of February 21, 1971, during a game against Oklahoma City, a Boston Bruins farm club. Kansas City was leading 2-1 with one minute to play when Plasse's mates were assessed a penalty. When Oklahoma City pulled its goalie, Plasse was facing a six-on-four situation. "They were really putting it to us, believe me," Plasse explains. Since he wasn't getting much help from his beleaguered teammates, Plasse had to do it all. "They threw the puck into our end from center, and when it came right to me, I skated out a bit—maybe ten feet—and flipped it down the ice." The Montreal native watched as the puck zipped into the enemy net, making him the envy of anyone who has ever taken his place in the goal crease as a hockey team's last line of defense.

Who Was College Football's Heisman Trophy Named After?

The Heisman Trophy, awarded by the New York City Downtown Athletic Club to the nation's outstanding college football player, was named after Johann Wilhelm Heisman. Heisman, a descendant of a German baron, was a great college football coach, and one of the game's great innovators. After playing tackle for Brown and the University of Pennsylvania, Heisman went on to compile a 186-70 coaching record for no less than eight schools—Akron, Auburn, Clemson, Georgia Tech, Penn, Rice, Oberlin, and Washington & Jefferson.

Heisman coached for sixteen years at Georgia Tech, where, in 1916, his Rambling Wrecks beat Cumberland College of Tennessee by a score of 222-0, the biggest rout of all time. Although Heisman obviously knew what he was doing, it is doubtful that his coaching philosophy would go over well with today's players. He believed that a coach "should be masterful and commanding, even dictatorial; he must be severe, arbitrary and little short of a czar." Heisman's win-or-else attitude was demonstrated to the fullest in 1894, when he employed a ringer in a game against Ohio State. The ringer quarterbacked the Akron squad, and his name was Johann Wilhelm Heisman.

Heisman was one of the first men to attempt to incorporate the forward pass into the game. In 1895, he observed a desperate North Carolina punter escape a big loss by throwing the ball—and completing it for a touchdown. Heisman was disgusted with the violent aspect of football, and saw the forward pass as a way to add some finesse to the sport. Also, Heisman invented the center snap and the scoreboard.

Upon retiring from coaching, Heisman became athletic director at the New York City Downtown Athletic Club, and the Heisman Trophy was born a year before his death.

What Is the Difference Between Men's and Women's Lacrosse?

Although men's lacrosse owes its heritage to North America, the women's game has its roots in England at the turn of the 20th century. It was introduced by British sports instructors and first played by women in English private schools.

The difference between the men's and women's games follows the difference in their respective histories. The men's game, rooted in the 1860s, was derived from an original version of American Indian "tribal warfare." The women's adaptation was a greatly modified version which then was imported to England. In lacrosse, women perceived the possibilities of a game of high skill. Their idea was to eliminate the physical aspect of the men's game and turn it into one of speed and skill.

Who Was the First Person Ever to Swim the English Channel?

Captain Matthew Webb, 1875. An Englishman, Webb stroked through the 21-mile-stretch between Cape Gris-Nez in France and Dover, England, despite the icy water. By 1926 five men had successfully completed the swim.

On August 6, 1926, a stocky nineteen-year-old New Yorker plunged into the Channel. Fourteen hours and 31 minutes later, Gertrude "Trudy" Ederle, the first woman to ever complete the ordeal, clambered out on the English coast, after having set a new record for the swim.

Ironically, just hours after her feat, Miss Ederle was cross-examined by a customs official in Dover, who demanded to see her passport and wondered where she had come from and what means of transportation she had used to reach Britain from France. It took a score of Gertrude's fans to persuade the vigilant customs men that she had, in fact, crossed the Channel by self-propulsion.

Which Boxer Was the First to Knock Down Muhammad Ali in a Championship Bout?

Joe Frazier, March 8, 1971. Boxing experts consider the first Frazier-Ali bout at Madison Square Garden the most widely touted fight since Jack Dempsey had his return match with Gene Tunney. The flamboyant Ali served as a catalyst for the hullabaloo, providing his usual assortment of predictions and taunts against his foe. "Frazier will fall in six," the former Cassius Clay boasted. Frazier was less offensive; until he got into the ring.

By the fourth round Ali's nose was bloodied, and he had begun to realize that he was in for a real fight. So was Frazier. Ali had punished Joe so often about the eyes that both were puffed by the sixth round. Still, neither fighter appeared willing to give an inch, although Ali appeared to have Frazier in trouble in the tenth round. However, Joe counterattacked in the eleventh and nearly put Ali away; the bell saving him and his rubbery legs. The respite helped Ali and he retaliated effectively enough to open cuts around Frazier's mouth. As the fighters rose for the 15th and final round it was a toss-up as to who was leading on points, although many experts leaned toward Frazier. As Ali rushed out and assaulted his stubborn foe, Frazier held fast and released a mighty left that delivered Ali to the canvas for the first knockdown of his career. It wasn't a knockout, though, and Ali rebounded, hoping to dispose of Frazier. They slugged to a finish and Frazier was awarded the decision as heavyweight champion.

Who Did Jack Dempsey Defeat to Win His First Heavyweight Championship?

Jess Willard. On July 4, 1919, Dempsey, a 24-year-old brawler from the gold-mining town of Manassa, Colorado, took on the then heavyweight champion, Jess Willard, a onetime Kansas farmboy who had grown cocky with his questionable title.

Willard had won the crown in 1916 from Jack Johnson in a controversial bout following which charges circulated that Johnson had "dumped" the bout to "The Great White Hope." Nevertheless, Willard was considered more than an adequate fighter. What's more, he stood an impressive 6-6, 260 pounds, while Dempsey weighed in at 6-1, 182 pounds.

"Dempsey will come rushing at me," Willard predicted in Toledo, Ohio, just before the fight, "I'll stick out my left. He'll run into it. Then I'll come in with a right uppercut and it'll be all over in the first round."

But Dempsey savagely floored Willard six times in the opening round, reducing the once confident champion to a bloody pulp. Willard was so badly belabored in rounds two and three that one observer said he looked like "an ox that was being butchered alive and on the hoof." Mercifully, Willard failed to answer the bell for the fourth round and Dempsey became the new heavyweight champion.

Which NBA Player Got into Three On-Court Fights During the 1976 Playoffs?

Hockey isn't the only sport that features "policemen." Basketball has its enforcers, too. First-year guard Ricky

Sobers established himself as the "blue knight" of the Phoenix Suns in the 1976 National Basketball Association playoffs, when he engaged in three fights—one in each playoff round.

First, the 6-3 Sobers slugged it out with 7-2½ center Tom Burleson of the Seattle Supersonics in the quarter-finals. Next, he demolished Golden State Warriors' forward Rick Barry with a sledgehammer shot in the mouth in the first half of the seventh and deciding game of the Suns' Eastern Conference playoff final. The rookie's decision over the 6-7 veteran superstar sparked his teammates, who turned from toads to tigers and outplayed the Warriors for the rest of the evening.

"I don't think of myself as leading the league in fights," Sobers explains. "I like to think of myself as leading the league in gaining respect." In layman's terms, "gaining respect" is a euphemism for knocking your opponent senseless so he won't bother you for the rest of the game.

Sobers' most one-sided victory came against Kevin Stacom, a 6-3 guard with the Boston Celtics. At last, he had picked on someone his own size. "Sobers is not afraid of anyone," said *Boston Globe* columnist Bob Ryan, who witnessed the fight. "He'll start a fight regardless of race, creed, color, national origin, size, or amount of facial hair. He could start a fight at a team party."

True or False: Until Julius Erving Repeated as the ABA's Scoring Champion in 1973-74, the League Had a Different High Scorer Each Year.

True. Starting in 1967-68 they included: Connie Hawkins, Pittsburgh Pipers; Rick Barry, Washington Capitals; Spencer Haywood, Denver Rockets; Dan Issel, Kentucky Colonels; Charlie Scott, Virginia Squires, and Erving, Virginia Squires.

How Did the Chicago White Sox Become Black Sox?

Angry because they considered themselves underpaid and abused by owner Charles Comiskey, members of the talented Chicago White Sox arranged to throw the 1919 World Series against the Cincinnati Reds. When court hearings established that the Chicago club had, in fact, worked out a "fix" on the Series, an enraged public dubbed them the Black Sox. Those involved in the Series-dumping were banned from baseball for life. Among the most prominent Chicago players was "Shoeless" Joe Jackson, an enormously popular and talented hitter. When Jackson emerged from the courthouse after delivering his confession of the fix, he was met on the steps by an incredulous newsboy who had been a diehard White Sox fan. With tears in his eyes, he looked up at Jackson and uttered the deathless line: "Say it ain't so, Joe!" But, alas, it was and the 1919 White Sox were, forever, to be known as the Black Sox. Their sad story later was to be told in a brilliant book called *Nine Men Out*.

Who Was the Big-Time Gambler Involved in the Black Sox Scandal? Name the Boxing Champion Who Was His Sidekick?

The gambler was Arnold Rothstein. Newspapers called him a "sportsman." His father called him a hoodlum. Whatever his moniker, Rothstein put together a fortune at two gambling dens in Manhattan. He mixed with such luminaries as oil magnates Joshua Cosden and Harry Sinclair, not to mention Charles Stoneham, owner of the New York Giants.

Rothstein's entourage included Abe Attell, who for twelve years had been world featherweight champion. He fought 365 fights and was never knocked out, losing only six times. Attell was the contact when Billy Maharg and his partner, Bill Burns, met in 1919 at Jamaica Racetrack to outline the proposition that would rock the sports world.

What Five Members of the 1969 World Champion New York Jets Were Involved in the Dramatic 1965 Orange Bowl?

New York Jets' quarterback Joe Namath, tight end Pete Lammons, wide receiver George Sauer, defensive tackle John Elliot, and defensive back Jim Hudson, all starters on the Jet squad that upset the Baltimore Colts in the 1969 Super Bowl, participated in the 1965 Orange Bowl, in which Texas beat Alabama 21-17.

Only Namath was on Bear Bryant's Alabama Crimson Tide; the other four were Texas Longhorns. Pete Lammons was a solid tight end for the Jets; he caught a critical TD pass from Namath in the AFL championship victory over Oakland which advanced New York to the Super Bowl. But in the Orange Bowl, Lammons was a key contributor to Namath's defeat as he intercepted two of Broadway Joe's passes while playing linebacker for the Longhorns. Jim Hudson was the Jets' strong safety and one of the most feared hitters in the league. At Texas, Hudson was also an outstanding offensive performer at wingback and quarterback. It was Hudson's 69-yard touchdown pass to George Sauer, one of Namath's favorite Jet receivers and one of the great pass catchers in the history of the AFL, that was the winning touchdown in the Longhorns' victory.

Which Player Performed for Each of the Following Teams: The Brooklyn Dodgers, New York Knicks, and New York Rangers?

Gladys Goodding. Originally the house organist at Madison Square Garden sporting events (especially Rangers hockey and Knickerbockers basketball), Miss Goodding eventually was hired to play the organ at Dodger home games in Ebbets Field. Hence, she played for the Dodgers, Knicks, and Rangers.

Who Was the Featured Female in the Tune "Take Me Out To The Ball Game."

Nelly Kelly. Written in 1908 by Jack Norworth (words) and Albert von Tilzer (music), the tune has remained a standard ever since. However, most fans are familiar only with the chorus, which never mentions Ms. Kelly. She did, however, receive much attention in the two introductions. To wit:

Nelly Kelly loved Base Ball games,
Knew the players, knew all their names,
You could see her there ev-'ry day,
Shout "Hurray"—when they'd play
Her boy friend by the name of Joe,
Said to Coney Isle, dear, let's go,
Then Nelly started to fret and pout,
And to him I heard her shout:
CHORUS

Nelly Kelly was sure some fan
She would root just like any man,
Told the Umpire he was wrong,
All along—good and strong
When the score was just two to two,
Nelly Kelly knew what to do,
Just to cheer up the boys she knew,
She made the gang sing this song:
CHORUS

How Did Baseball's World Series Develop?

Before the World Series came into being, major league baseball consisted of the National Baseball Federation (later the National League) and no challengers were on the horizon. But in 1901 an enterprising journalist named Ban Johnson and Charles Comiskey, a onetime player and manager, decided to organize their own league and compete with the National. Thus, the American League was born.

Wisely, it formulated harsh but effective rules of player conduct and raided the established league for players. Once it became apparent that public opinion favored the American League, owners of the National League recognized its existence; but only to a point. When the Boston Red Sox won the American League pennant in 1903 the Sox challenged the National League champion Pittsburgh Pirates. It would, the Sox insisted, be a true championship series. At first the Pirates' management refused the challenge, but the public insisted that it be played and, as a result, a best-of-nine World Series took place. The Red Sox won the series, five games to three, in a tremendous upset and in two years—no World Series was played in 1904 because of a dispute—the annual fall classic was here to stay.

Which Member of Baseball's Hall of Fame Was Fired Because He Admitted to Betting on Horses?

Rogers "The Rajah" Hornsby. In February 1944, Hornsby, one of the finest hitters in baseball history, took a job as manager of the Vera Cruz team in the Mexican League. Previously, Hornsby had been manager of the St. Louis Browns in the American League when Donald Barnes, owner of the club, asked Hornsby about betting on horses. "The Rajah," wrote Dave Egan in the *Boston Daily Record*, "made the usual answer, and appended the usual so-what-if-I-do. So he was fired forthwith . . . fired out of the life he had known for a quarter of a century because he had not been a hypocrite, and had not played it smart, and had not told smooth lies. He did not drink and did not smoke and could not lie even if his career depended upon a successful lie."

116

What Kentucky Derby Winner Produced the Highest Win Payoff?

Donerail produced the highest win price in Kentucky Derby history when he returned $184.90 on a $2 win bet in the 1913 Run for the Roses. It was with good reason that Donerail went to the post at such astronomical odds. The colt was still a maiden, having run only twice prior to Derby Day, finishing third both times. Furthermore, Donerail hadn't raced in months, having competed only as a two-year-old.

There was a heavy favorite in the race; Ten Point went off at even money. Ten Point, however, proved only second best, beaten a few feet by 91-1 Donerail. The upset was such a shocker that Donerail's jockey Roscoe Goose did not cash a single ticket, and the horse's owner had only a moderate bet.

What Was Hockey's Famous "Battle Of The Bulge"?

In 1947, 1948, and 1949 the Toronto Maple Leafs, coached by Clarence "Hap" Day and managed by Conn Smythe, had won an unprecedented three Stanley Cup championships, and naturally were favored to win again in 1950. But the vitriolic Smythe was worried. He was fearful that his players were becoming too complacent and too fat.

Smythe's fears were confirmed early in the 1949-50 season when the Leafs opened their campaign with all the vigor of a pricked balloon. Finally, on November 30, Smythe, a veteran of both World Wars, opened what became known as hockey's classic "Battle of the Bulge."

Headlines in the Toronto newspapers screamed the news: SMYTHE READS THE RIOT ACT TO LEAFS. Although Smythe singled out defenseman Garth Boesch and forwards Howie Meeker, Harry Watson, Vic Lynn, and Sid Smith for his blasts, the key target of Smythe's ire was his longtime goaltending stalwart, Walter "Turk" Broda.

Smythe's opening gun in "The Battle of the Bulge" was a demand that his players reduce their weight to specified limits. Broda, who weighed 197 pounds, was ordered to lose 7 pounds. To underline the seriousness of his offensive, Smythe promptly called up reserve goalie Gil Mayer from his Pittsburgh farm team. "We're starting Mayer in our next game," Smythe asserted, "and he'll stay in here even if the score is five hundred to one against the Leafs—and I don't think it will be."

This was the supreme insult to Broda, who, except for a stint in the army, had never missed a game during his twelve seasons as a Toronto goalie. But Smythe was unimpressed. It was Tuesday and he was giving Turk until Saturday to fulfill the demand.

Smythe's outburst reverberated across Canada and parts of the United States, and soon "The Battle of the Bulge" became a cause celebre. Neutral observers regarded Turk's tussle with the scales as a huge joke, win or lose, but to the Toronto boss it was no joke. None of the Leafs was particularly amused, either.

Toronto restaurant owner Sam Shopsowitz took an ad in the local papers, declaring, "For that 'Old Broda' look, eat at Shopsy's." Another featured a caricature of Broda stopping eight pucks at once with the caption: "Just three weeks ago I was the best goalkeeper in the league. If I'd only eaten a few more king-sized steaks at the Palisades I'd be fat enough to fill the whole net and they would never score on me!"

After one day of severe dieting, Turk trimmed his weight from 197 to 193 and all of Canada seemed to breathe easier. Even so, by midweek Broda had still not reached his approved weight limit and Smythe dropped another bombshell. He traded five players as well as cash "in five figures" to Cleveland for tall, twenty-three-year-old goalie Al Rollins. According to hockey experts, Rollins was the best professional goalie outside the National Hockey League.

Smythe had set the final weigh-in for Saturday afternoon, prior to the evening match against the New York Rangers at

Maple Leaf Gardens. One by one, the penitent Leafs stepped on the scales under Smythe's watchful eye. Watson, Boesch, Lynn, Smith, and Meeker all weighed in under the limit. Finally it was Broda's turn.

Turk moved forward and gingerly placed his feet on the platform. The numbers finally settled—just under 190 pounds. He had made it! If Turk was delighted, Smythe was doubly enthused because he regarded his goaltender with paternal affection. "There may be better goalies around somewhere," said the manager, "but there's no greater sportsman than the Turkey. If the Rangers score on him tonight, I should walk out and hand him a malted milk, just to show I'm not trying to starve him to death."

That night the Maple Leaf Gardens was packed with 13,359 Turk-rooters, and when the former fat man skated out for the opening face-off, the Gardens' regimental band swung into "Happy Days Are Here Again" and followed that with a chorus of "She's Too Fat for Me."

Finally, referee George Gravel dropped the puck to start the game, and the Rangers immediately swarmed in on Broda. This time, however, he was the Turk of old. "He never looked better," said Toronto *Globe and Mail* sports editor Jim Vipond. "He moved side to side in front of his netted bastion to block the best efforts of the Rangers."

Unfortunately, Broda's slimmer teammates couldn't beat goalie Chuck Rayner of the Rangers and the second period ended with the teams tied, 0-0.

Early in the third period the Leafs were attempting a change in lines when Howie Meeker and Vic Lynn, two of the marked fat men, combined to feed a lead pass to Max Bentley, who normally wouldn't have been on the ice with them. Bentley dipsy-doodled through the Ranger checkers and unleashed a steaming shot that flew past Rayner. Later in the period another fat man, Harry Watson, skimmed a pass to Bill Ezinicki, who beat Rayner.

Now all eyes were on the clock as it ticked toward the end of the game. With only a minute remaining, Broda still had a

shutout. The count-down began: ten, nine, eight seconds
—the crowd was on its feet—seven, six, five—they were
roaring as if the Leafs had won the Stanley Cup—four, three,
two, one. The game was over! Turk dove for the puck and
gathered it in. It was his symbolic trophy for winning "The
Battle of the Bulge."

Which Teams Met in the First Intercollegiate Football Game Ever Played?

Rutgers and Princeton, November 6, 1869. Not only did
the two schools play the first intercollegiate football game,
but on the same day Princeton introduced the idea of a
cheering section.

The game was played at Rutgers, and to offset any possible
home field advantage some of the Princeton players decided
to unveil some new strategy. What they had in mind was a
basic form of what we now know as cheering. It was decided
that during the game the Princeton players would periodi-
cally let loose some heart-stopping yells intended to frighten
the opposition.

Although the Rutgers players were quite confused by their
opponents' continuous oral outbursts, Princeton's strategy
was unsuccessful. It seemed that it took too much breath,
attention, and energy to keep yelling, and the exhausted
Princeton players were also confusing themselves with all the
noise. The end result of the Princeton experiment was that a
startled but breathful Rutgers team downed a hell-raising
breathless Princeton squad, 6-4.

The yelling tactics employed by Princeton became known
as "the scarer," and played an important role in the rematch
between the two schools. When the teams got together again,
the Princeton squad was accompanied by a group of students
who agreed to yell "the scarer" so the players could concen-
trate on playing, which they did. Princeton won 8-0, and
since then all college and some professional teams employ
cheerleaders to yell "scarers" at the opposition.

When Was the First Time an Instant Replay Reversed the Result of an Already Completed Football Game?

November 16, 1940. Dartmouth vs. Cornell. At the conclusion of the game Cornell defeated Dartmouth 7-3. However, it appeared obvious to everyone except the game's referee, Red Friesell, that Cornell had won, thanks to a "fifth down" they were awarded in the final seconds of the game. Let's reconstruct the events leading up to the "fifth down."

With one minute left to play Cornell had the ball, first and goal, on the Dartmouth 6 yard line. Dartmouth was leading 3-0. On first down Cornell running back Mort Landsberg drove through the middle for a gain of three yards, placing the ball on the Dartmouth 3 yard line.

There were 45 seconds remaining. Quarterback Walt Scholl ran inside for two yards to the Dartmouth one.

With twenty seconds remaining Cornell would have two cracks to win from the one yard line. On third down, Landsberg went up the middle again but was stopped cold after gaining only two inches. Now Cornell would be faced with a fourth down situation, with only ten seconds left to play.

At this time Cornell Coach Carl Snavely sent a substitute in to stop the clock. Unfortunately the move backfired since Cornell had exceeded its timeouts and consequently was penalized five yards.

It was now fourth and goal on the 6 yard line. Scholl dropped back to pass and threw into the end zone, where the ball was batted down by Dartmouth defensive back Ray Hall. Three seconds remained in the game and the ball belonged to Dartmouth.

At least that's the way it looked when Referee Friesell took the ball and started walking toward the Dartmouth 20 yard line. However, head linesman Joe McKenny had detected a Cornell offside and he informed Friesell of this. Under ordinary circumstances, Dartmouth would be asked if they accepted or declined the penalty, which they would have declined, of course. But for some strange reason, Friesell took the ball and returned it to the Dartmouth 6 yard line, and signaled fourth down for Cornell once again.

Dartmouth captain Lou Young raced after Friesell pleading with him to listen, that he'd made a mistake. Young's pleas fell upon deaf ears, and Cornell snapped their infamous fifth down. Scholl passed for a touchdown to halfback Bill Murphy and with the extra point Cornell won, 7-3.

Two days later, Red Friesell reported his error to ECAC commissioner Asa Bushnell. He had examined the game films and down charts and admitted to awarding Cornell a fifth down. The evidence was incontrovertible.

In one of the most gentlemanly displays of all amateur and professional sports, James Lynah, Cornell's athletic director, upon learning of the referee's admitted error and its validity based on the game films, wired Dartmouth officials relinquishing Cornell's claim to the victory.

How Long Was the Jack Dempsey-Gene Tunney "Long Count"?

According to film records, 14 seconds. The extraordinary event took place on September 22, 1927, a year after Tunney had won the heavyweight championship from Dempsey in Philadelphia's Municipal Stadium. This time the fight was held in Soldier's Field, Chicago, before 105,000 fans.

The quick-punching Tunney was leading the fight until the seventh round when Dempsey scored with a hard left to Tunney's jaw, and followed it with a flurry of hard lefts and rights until Gene collapsed to the canvas. As the referee was about to start the count, he realized that the overzealous Dempsey had failed to retreat to a neutral corner—according to the rules—so the count was delayed until the challenger finally moved away from the champion. At the count of "nine," Tunney clambered to his feet and eluded Dempsey's attempted knockout blow.

Having regained his composure and senses, Tunney rallied and blasted Dempsey as he had in the opening fight. The agile champ retained his crown, and Dempsey could only lament the fact that he might have won the title back if only he had been less exuberant and had gone to his corner. Tunney, however, offered the squelch, asserting that he could have lifted himself up any time he wanted to resume the fight.

Name Five Boxing Movies.

While baseball movies have, for the most part, fallen into the mainstream of romanticized film fare, boxing films have been concerned with hard-hitting subject matter, providing symbolic backdrops for moral issues and soul-searching. This was evident in such Hollywood productions as *Golden Boy* with William Holden; *Body And Soul*, with John Garfield; *The Champion*, starring Kirk Douglas; *The Harder They Fall*, with Humphrey Bogart; and *Somebody Up There Likes Me* with Paul Newman. One of the most popular boxing films was *Rocky*, starring Sylvester Stallone, a virtual unknown when filmed, which went on to win an Academy Award.

Which Famous Sportscaster Publicly Apologized on the Air for Downgrading the St. Louis Browns?

Bill Stern. During the 1944 baseball season Stern was doing a daily sports program on the National Broadcasting Company network. On one show Stern opined that the Browns might not win the pennant unless they tried harder. A torrent of criticism poured into Stern's office, including objections from club owner Don Barnes and Jimmy Conzelman, a football coach who then was affiliated with the American League baseball team. Barnes and numerous friends withered Stern. "They told me in no uncertain terms," said Stern, "how wrong I'd been, how injudicious

123

in my choice of words. I immediately aired a formal apology and appreciated the lesson."

The Browns confirmed the lesson by winning the American League pennant that year.

Name the Evangelist Who Also Was a Top-Flight Baseball Star?

Billy Sunday. Before turning to a career on the pulpit as the Reverend Billy Sunday, he was a superb outfielder with the Chicago White Stockings. Many observers credited Sunday with helping Chicago win the pennant in 1886. It all happened in a crucial game between Detroit and Chicago with the White Stockings holding a slim lead over their opponents.

Detroit had two men on base with two out and catcher Charley Bennett at the plate. The pitch was just where Bennett wanted it and he slammed the ball toward very deep right field. Sunday, who was considered the fastest man in both leagues, turned and ran in the direction of the ball. He leaped over a bench on the lip of the outfield and continued running. As he made his way, Sunday talked out loud: "Oh, God. If you're going to help me, come on now!" At this point Sunday leaped in the air and threw up his hand. He nabbed the ball and fell on his back. Thanks to Sunday, Chicago won the game and, eventually, the pennant.

Sunday enjoyed telling friends that he played for two teams, the White Stocking and "God's team." When asked how he got on God's team, Billy would explain: "I walked down a street in Chicago with some ballplayers, and we went into a saloon. It was Sunday afternoon and we got tanked up and then went and sat down on a curbing. Across the street a company of men and women were playing on instruments—horns, flutes and slide trombones—and the others were singing the gospel hymns that I used to hear my mother sing back in the log cabin in Iowa and back in the old church where I used to go to Sunday school. I arose and said to the boys, 'I'm through. I am going to Jesus Christ. We've come to the parting of the ways.' "

Although his teammates needled him, Sunday followed the Salvation Army singers into the Pacific Garden Restaurant Mission on Van Buren Street. Billy may not have known it at the time but he was on his way to the Sawdust Trail where, as he put it, he would emerge as the scrappiest antagonist that "blazing-eyed, eleven-hoofed, forked-tail old Devil" ever had to go against.

What Is Codeball?

The obscure sport of codeball was invented in the late 1920s by—who else?—Dr. William Code. The game attained the acme of its popularity in the 1930s, and was recommended as part of the armed forces sports program during World War II.

There are two vastly different styles of codeball, an outdoors version and an indoors game. The latter is called "codeball-in-the-court," and features the same rules as handball, except that instead of using one's hands, the player must use his feet. The ball must be kicked on the fly or on the first bounce off the court walls. Only when preparing to serve is a player permitted to touch the ball with his hands.

The outdoor game is called "codeball-on-the-green." This version is played on a field similar to a golf course. In outdoor codeball, one must kick the ball from its starting place on a tee, over the variously distanced holes, to the green, where sits an inverted cone-shaped bowl with an opening 18 inches wide. As in golf, the player who completes the course, which is 14 holes, in the least number of "strokes" is the winner.

Codeball-in-the-court was Dr. Code's original game, but the outdoor game was invented because the indoor version was too difficult for senior citizens.

By the early 1930s, codeball-in-the-court facilities appeared in playgrounds in Chicago, Todedo, Dayton, Fort Wayne, and Louisville, among others. Codeball-on-the-green had been introduced to many golf courses and summer camps.

In 1933, the first national codeball-in-the-court championships were held at the University of Michigan. The winner was George Webster of Chicago, who won the championship four times in the ten-year history of the tournament. Webster is regarded as the greatest codeball-in-the-court player of all time. The tournament was discontinued after 1942, because of the wartime-imposed difficulty in obtaining pure rubber for codeballs.

A codeball-on-the-green championship tourney was held annually from 1935 to 1939. Joseph Sicking, who won the title in 1938 and 1939, holds the record for the best round of codeball-on-the-green with a 63.

Dr. Code's finest hour occurred in 1952, when a demonstration of codeball-on-the-green was staged at the Olympic Village in Helsinki, Finland, prior to the 1952 Olympic Games. Representatives of several nations expressed interest in the game, but the sport has yet to be added to the Olympics' repertoire.

Who Is the Only Man to Win the Olympic Long-Distance Triple—the 5,000 and 10,000 Meters, and the 26-Mile Marathon?

Emil Zatopek of Czechoslovakia. Zatopek had not run competitively until he was 18 years old. But in the 1948 Olympics, Zatopek was first under the wire in the 5,000 meters.

Zatopek's victory in 1948 was just a scant preview of things to come. In the 1952 Olympics, the Czech army officer repeated as 5,000 meter champ, and also won the gold in the 10,000 meters. Despite the fact that Zatopek had never

127

before attempted the grueling marathon, he decided to go for the triple. Also entered in the marathon was Jim Peters of Great Britain, considered the world's premier marathoner. So it was just natural that Zatopek, when seeking advice on how to approach the marathon, went to the world's best. Peters told Zatopek to be sure to pace himself carefully. So Zatopek followed Peters' advice and paced himself—but unfortunately for Peters, the Czech, still unsure of exactly how fast to go, stayed step for step with the Englishman. A little past the halfway mark, Zatopek informed Peters that he wanted to quicken the pace. So Peters went faster to keep up with the Czech, but the pace still wasn't fast enough for Zatopek. Finally, Peters succumbed to the torrid pace and had to drop out of the race. Emil Zatopek went on to win the marathon in Olympic record time, and become the only winner of the long-distance triple crown.

Hockey's Greatest Scorer, Gordie Howe, Had a Younger Brother Who Also Reached the Big Leagues. Who Was He?

Victor Stanley Howe. If Gordie Howe was one of the National (and World) Hockey League's outstanding success stories, Gordie's brother Vic suffered the opposite fate. Built along Gordie's generous dimensions, Vic was developed in the New York Rangers' farm system. The Broadway Blueshirts had dreams that Vic, who was a year-and-a-half younger than Gordie, would also become a superstar. Twice Vic, also a right wing, was promoted to the NHL Rangers, in 1950-51 and a period from 1953 through 1955. At the very least, Vic was a consummate failure. He seemed to lack Gordie's fire and, although he possessed skills as a skater and shooter the younger Howe never seemed able to get them to jell in his favor. He soon was demoted and eventually retired to private life. Conversely, more than 20 years after Vic left the majors, Gordie still was a star; this time playing alongside his sons, Mark and Marty, on the Houston Aeros.

Who Was the Youngest Player in Pro Basketball History?

Eighteen-year-old Joe Grabowski, Chicago Stags. When Grabowski went directly from high school to the NBA, two years after the league was organized, he was three months short of his 19th birthday. Apparently age had little to do with his ability since Grabowski remained a professional star for several years.

By contrast, the oldest player was Bob Cousy, who temporarily came out of retirement—he was coach of the Cincinnati Royals—during the 1969-70 season to show his men how to move the ball. At age 43 Cousy lasted seven games before packing it in.

Who Was the Fastest Baseball Player Never to Have Played in the Major Leagues?

James Thomas "Cool Papa" Bell. At his peak in the thirties when black players were unable to play in either the American or National Leagues, Bell showed his speed in the Negro National League, the Mexican League, and the Cuban League, among others. Those who played with and against Bell claimed he was the original Kid Lightning on the basepaths. "That man," said pitcher Satchel Paige, a Hall of Famer, "was so fast he could turn out the light and jump in bed before the room got dark." Observers insist that Bell was faster than Ty Cobb, Lou Brock, Jackie Robinson, and even Jesse Owens, one of America's greatest Olympic stars. During a 200-game season in 1933, Bell stole 175 bases. It was not unusual for Bell to score from first base *on a sacrifice*. In a 1934 East-West All-Star Game, he scored from second on a ground ball to win the game, 1-0. "They once timed me," said Bell, "circling the bases in 12 seconds flat." Pepper Martin, star base-runner of the "Gashouse Gang" St. Louis Cardinals, credited Bell with teaching him how to improve his base-stealing.

Which Major League Ball Park Has a Special Ground Rule for Pigeons?

Fenway Park, Boston. The home of the Red Sox is responsible for a unique ground rule that regulates the play of a ball if the horsehide hits a pigeon in mid-air. According to the regulation if a batted ball hits a flying pigeon the umpire must rule the ball dead. It is not known if the pigeons have a rule to cover *their* splattering of either balls or players.

Which Two Pitchers Stopped Joe DiMaggio's Consecutive Game Hitting Streak at 56 Games?

Al Smith and Jim Bagby. The Cleveland Indians faced the Yankees in a night game on July 17, 1941, before 67,468 fans at Cleveland. A day earlier DiMaggio, alias "The Yankee Clipper," had produced three hits to extend his streak to 56 games. To thwart Joe the Indians came up with left-handed Smith, one of the better pitchers in the American League.

It looked like DiMaggio would come through on his first at bat; he whacked a hot ground ball along the third base line, but the Indians' Ken Keltner stabbed the ball and pegged out DiMaggio. The second time up Joe D. was walked. For his third trip, DiMaggio duplicated his first blow and, again, Keltner was the culprit, nabbing the ball and tossing Joe out at first.

But DiMaggio would get one more opportunity; in the eighth inning with a runner on first. Cleveland's player-manager Lou Boudreau, who played shortstop, had brought in Jim Bagby, a right-handed knuckleballer, as relief pitcher, and DiMaggio responded with an erratically bouncing grounder to deep short. Boudreau got to the ball and converted it into a double-play and the Clipper's streak had ended. DiMaggio had managed a hit in every game for more than two months, breaking the old record by 15.

Who Are the Only Heavyweights Ever to Knock Out Joe Louis?

Max Schmeling, then the heavyweight champion, KO'd the Brown Bomber in his first attempt at the title, June 19, 1936, at Yankee Stadium. This was the match that was to set the stage for the dramatic one-round KO of Schmeling by Louis two years later at the Stadium.

However, it was more than fifteen years before Louis was to taste the canvas again! The slayer this time was none other than Rocky Marciano, who knocked out Louis in the eighth round at Madison Square Garden in New York on October 26, 1951, and later was to claim the title.

In fact, this was one of the most tragic fights in the history of boxing, and might never have taken place if it weren't for the corruption and greed which permeated the sport in the early fifties. Louis was persuaded by James Norris, the czar of boxing, to make a comeback. Although his initial attempt ended miserably, losing to champion Ezzard Charles, Norris convinced Louis that he still could make a return to the ring. He tried—and failed—with Marciano. Barney Nagler, the famed boxing historian, tells the story:

"Rocky Marciano, unbeaten and untied, was managed by Al Weill, who doubled in sheer brass as Norris' matchmaker. Weill's duality was in direct violation of the rules of the New York State Athletic Commission, but Norris shut his eyes to this. It was easy for Norris to prevail upon Weill to permit Louis to fight Marciano.

"Louis was 37 years old and only a shadow of his former self. His reflexes were gone, and it was sheer cruelty to send him into the ring against Marciano. But the match was made.

"The end came in the eighth round. It was effected not by Marciano's powerful right hand but by his left hook. Short and to the point, the hook landed on Louis' baldish head. He went down and took an 8 count. When he rose, Marciano pinned him on the ropes and hit him with two more left hooks before launching the last punch of the fight, a right to the jaw that sent Louis through the ropes onto the ring apron, where he lay with one leg inside the ropes. Sugar Ray Robinson, who had gained many glorious victories in the same arena, was in a ringside seat. When Louis went down for the first time, he sensed the inevitable conclusion of it all and began moving toward the ring. And when the end came he jumped into the ring and consoled Louis, who had fought for the last time.''

Why Couldn't a Hockey Goaltender Leave His Feet in the Early Days of the Ice Game?

Because if he did—he'd receive a two-dollar fine! If he did it a second time in the same game he'd receive an additional three-dollar levy and a five-minute major penalty to boot! Of course, if that rule were still in effect today, goalies would lead the league in penalty minutes.

Name the Only Professional Hockey Goalie Who Refuses to Wear a Protective Face Mask.

Andy Brown ignored the face guard through the '76-'77 season. "I just don't feel right in one," said Brown, who also races automobiles in the off-season. "I can't get comfortable with it. I tried one a few years ago, but I could never get used to it." Brown said that without the mask he has received about 200 stitches and lost all of his front teeth "but nothing serious."

Who Is the Only Hockey Player Who Wore an Egyptian Ring and a Pendant in His Ear?

Howie Young, formerly of the Phoenix Roadrunners of the Western Hockey League. He also believes in extraterrestrial life, owns two motorcycles, and once wore a wig in a game.

Which Baseball Slugger Camped at an Editor's Doorstep to Register a Beef?

Jeff Heath, Cleveland Indians. A sensitive soul, Heath, who was a member of the Boston Braves' 1948 pennant winners, was offended by a story written about him in the *Sporting News*. The story so bothered Heath (often called "Lord Jeff") that he decided to stop off at the conclusion of the season to see the *Sporting News'* publisher, Taylor Spink, as he drove home to Washington State. "I just wanted Taylor to know my side of the story," said Heath.

Unfortunately, Heath's timing was poor. He crossed the Mississippi River into Downtown St. Louis at six in the morning. "I decided," said Heath, "that the only thing I could do was to drive to the *Sporting News* building and sleep in the car until Mister Spink came to work. I assumed that that would be around nine or ten in the morning. I drove to his office, parked and tried to sleep, but I was uneasy, afraid some guy might come down the street and steal my expensive shoes. So, a few minutes after seven, I locked the car and went to see if I could get into the building to doze off. Maybe there'd be a night watchman or janitor. The door was unlocked. I climbed the stairs and whom did I meet but Spink, himself!"

Who Was the Greatest Small Man in Professional Basketball?

Bob Cousy, Boston Celtics, 6-1, 175 pounds. Playing for Red Auerbach's Celtics, Cousy remained at the top of the heap for 13 seasons. "Cousy," said Larry Fox of the New York *Daily News*, "certainly is the greatest of the little men. He starred in a game in which he stood no more than chest high against many of his rivals."

A graduate of New York's playgrounds, Cousy became an ace with Holy Cross. In 1949 and 1950 he was All-America with the Crusaders. In 1950-51 he was voted rookie-of-the-year in the National Basketball Association and was an NBA

All-Star ten times in his 13-year career. "Also," says Fox, "he sparked the Celtics to a league domination almost unparalleled in sports."

Who Was the Best Little Tennis Player in History?

Bryan "Bitsy" Grant. At five feet, four inches tall, Grant alternately was known as the "Mighty Atom" and the "Giant Killer," and for good reason. In 1933, Grant defeated Ellsworth Vines when Vines was the top-ranked player in the world, after winning Forest Hills and Wimbledon.

Grant's titles included the National Clay Court, the Eastern Grass Court, the Texas, and Western Championships. Grant was ranked among the top ten in the United States throughout the nineteen-thirties.

After a World War II stint in the United States Armed Forces, Grant returned to the courts and in 1955 won the National Senior Clay Court Singles championship, defeating Jack Staton, 6-0, 6-4. Appropriately, Grant won the title in the stadium built and named in his honor by the City of Atlanta.

Who Was the Canadian-Born Pitcher Who Pinch Hit a Base Hit in His First Major League at Bat?

Oscar Judd. A farm boy from Rebecca, Ontario, Judd could hit as well as he could pitch and proved it by being named to the 1943 American League All-Star Team. After seven outstanding minor league seasons, he was promoted to the Boston Red Sox. It was Boston manager Joe Cronin who sent Judd up against the great Bob Feller whereupon Oscar came through.

Once his pitching arm came up lame, Judd, a slow-talking, fast-running Canadian, made a comeback in the National League before drifting down to the Toronto Maple Leafs of the International League. Despite his lingering arm trouble, Judd took the mound on May 4, 1949 for Toronto before 22,206 fans at Maple Leaf Stadium, Toronto's biggest opening day baseball crowd, prior, of course, to the Blue Jays' debut. He held the strong Newark Bears to three hits in eight innings as the Leafs won, 4-3. The following year he retired.

How Did the Pitcher Leroy Paige Get the Nickname "Satchel"?

The greatest of all black pitchers (before blacks were freely allowed to pitch in the majors), Paige was not nicknamed "Satchel" because of a penchant for carrying shopping bags. He did, however, receive the nickname because of the size of his feet.

Others who watched him pitch believe his nickname should have been "Whizbang." Joe DiMaggio declared Paige the fastest pitcher he ever saw and in the thirties and forties, Satchel bested Dizzy Dean in six out of eight exhibition games and beat Bob Feller in his prime. Finally, in 1948, when he was said to be 42 years old (although others insist that Paige was older), he signed with Bill Veeck's Cleveland Indians and pitched superbly. He later pitched for the St. Louis Browns until 1953, always dispensing cheery homilies. ("Don't look back—something may be gaining on you!") Eventually, he was admitted to the Baseball Hall of Fame, but he never quit the game. In 1977 he served as pitching coach for New Orleans in the American Association and pitched batting practice. Asked his age, Paige replied: "Somewhere between 85 and 100!"

Who Was the Author and Where Did His Poem "Casey At The Bat" First Appear?

Ernest Lawrence Thayer's classic baseball poem was published in the *San Francisco Examiner* on June 3, 1888. A portion of the poem follows:

There was ease in Casey's manner as he stepped into his place.

There was pride in Casey's bearing and a smile lit CASEY'S face.

And when, responding to the cheers, he lightly doffed his hat,

No stranger in the crowd could doubt 'twas Casey at the bat, "Strike one," the umpire said.

From the benches dark with people there went up a muffled roar,

Like the beating of the stormwaves on a stern but distant shore.

With a smile of Christian charity great Casey's visage shone;

He stilled the rising tumult, he bade the game go on.

Oh, somewhere in this favored land the sun is shining bright;

The band is playing somewhere and somewhere hearts are light;

And somewhere men are laughing and little children shout;

But there is no joy in Mudville, great Casey has just struck out.

Which Notable Double-Play Combination Was Immortalized in Poetry by Author Franklin Pierce Adams?

The Chicago Cubs' combination of Tinker, Evers, and Chance. Usually, the double-play began with a ground ball to shortstop Tinker, who relayed the ball to second baseman Evers, who then pegged the ball to first baseman Chance.

In his poem, "Baseball's Sad Lexicon," Adams penned the following:

Ruthlessly pricking our gunfalon bubble,

Making a Giant hit into a double,

Words that are weighty with nothing but trouble:

"Tinker to Evers to Chance."

What Thoroughbred Won the Most Races in American Racing History?

Kingston. Kingston won an incredible 89 races in his nine years of racing. As a three-year-old in 1887, Kingston won thirteen out of eighteen races, finishing out of the money only once. He would not finish out of the money again until he was nine years old. Between off-the-board finishes, Kingston raced eighty times, winning 61 times. The son of Spendthrift and foal of Kapanga finally was retired after winning four, and not finishing out of the money in nine starts, as a ten-year-old.

Which Boxing Champion Inspired a Night Club to Build a Dance Floor to Simulate a Boxing Ring, and Which Politician Threw His Hat Into That Ring?

Retired lightweight champion Benny Leonard inspired his brother to open a night place in New York called "The Ringside." The dance floor was arranged to appear like a boxing ring. In the spring of 1925, when it appeared that New York's ailing Mayor John Hylan would not run again, Jimmy "Beau James" Walker became a favorite to succeed Hylan (which he later did). One night at The Ringside, Benny Leonard got into the ring and introduced celebrities, among them S. Jay Kaufman, one of Walker's close friends. Kaufman went on to say, "And I now have the great honor of introducing to you my friend, Jimmy Walker—the next mayor of the City of New York."

Walker rose. "I accept the nomination," he said. "My friend Jay Kaufman has had this idea for a long time. He has talked to a great many people about it—mostly the wrong people. But he has the theory that if enough people keep talking about it, the right people will begin to believe that it is a good idea."

Not long after that Jimmy Walker won the nomination.

In His First College Game at Madison Square Garden, Bill Bradley of Princeton Faced Cazzie Russell of Michigan. How Did Bradley Both Win and Lose the Battle on December 30, 1964?

All of the New York newspapers played up the confrontation between Bradley and Russell as if it was to be the battle of the century. Headlines roared: KEY TEST . . . BRADLEY OR CAZZIE? SHOWDOWN AT HAND! Bradley responded by scoring 41 points. Russell scored 27 points. But with four minutes and 37 seconds remaining, Bradley committed his fifth personal foul and left the game. Later Bradley was chosen as the game's most valuable player, but the individual effort was overshadowed by the fact that Russell's Michigan team won the game by one basket.

Bradley continued starring for Princeton and on March 20, 1965, in a game against Wichita, Bradley played what many consider his greatest game as a collegian, as Princeton won 118-82.

Who Was the Rhode Island State Defensive Star Who Helped Upset Favored Bowling Green in the 1946 National Invitation Tournament?

Ernie Calverly. Bowling Green was winning the game thanks to behemoth Don Otten. But with three minutes and 20 seconds remaining, Otten committed his fifth personal foul and was ejected from the game. Rhode Island trailed, 70-72, with a minute and ten seconds remaining when Calverly took aim from a point near the center stripe and fired a long shot that sailed straight through the hoop.

However, Bowling Green again took a two-point lead and with two seconds remaining Rhode Island took possession of the ball out of bounds at mid-floor. Calverly received the ball in the backcourt. He had no time for a pass or a play. A score seemed impossible, yet he managed to sink a field goal to send the game into overtime. Rhode Island then outscored

Bowling Green eight to five, and Calverly froze the ball with a minute-and-a-half remaining to give his team the victory.

How Many Baseball Players Have Participated in Games in Four Different Decades? Who Was the Most Recent?

Minnie Minoso was the 14th and most recent big-leaguer to have played in four different decades. The others were Nick Altrock (1898-1933), Dan Brouthers (1879-1904), Eddie Collins (1906-1930), Kid Gleason (1888-1912), Jim McGuire (1884-1912), Bobo Newsom (1929-1953), Jack O'Connor (1887-1910), Jim O'Rourke (1876-1904), John Picus Quinn (1909-1933), John B. Ryan (1889-1913), Mickey Vernon (1939-1960), Ted Williams (1939-1960), Early Wynn (1939-1963), Minnie Minoso (1949-1976).

Name the Big Three Pitchers Who Powered the St. Louis Browns to Their 1944 American League Pennant?

Denny Galehouse, Nelson Potter, and Bob Muncrief. The Browns, who eventually transferred to Baltimore in 1954, never won another pennant in St. Louis, but the 1944 team was a glorious edition backed by splendid pitching and the astute managing of James Luther Sewell. St. Louis finished atop the American League in 1944 with 89 wins against 65 losses. Galehouse (9-10), Potter (19-7) and Muncrief (13-8) were abetted by a few other solid hurlers including Sig Jakucki, Jack Kramer, and Sam Zoldak. Galehouse and Kramer won the Browns' two games in their 4-2 World Series loss to the St. Louis Cardinals. Muncrief was the loser in the Series' only extra-inning game (the second match won in the tenth inning) after coming in to relieve Potter in the seventh inning.

139

Who Was Responsible for the Best Rainy-Day Effort by a Professional Football Running Back?

Gale Sayers, Chicago Bears, 1965. Facing the San Francisco Forty-Niners at Wrigley Field in the last game of the season, the Bears were disturbed by a rainfall which began moments before the opening kick-off. The home team, coached by George Halas, figured that the rain would hamper the running game of rookie ace Sayers, who had led Chicago to eight straight victories and had scored 16 touchdowns, just four short of the National Football League's season record of 20. The visiting Forty-Niners were pleased, on the theory that rain would make it easier to stop the Bears' running game.

But the mud appeared to have no effect on Sayers' traction. Minutes after the opening kickoff, he scored an 80-yard touchdown. Then, with five minutes remaining in the second quarter, he scored again and four minutes later he made his third touchdown. Early in the third quarter Sayers scored his fourth touchdown and minutes later buzzed straight up the middle for his fifth TD.

Sayers was now just one score away from tying the one-game record of six touchdowns set 35 years earlier by Ernie Nevers of the Chicago Cardinals. But Coach Halas was more interested in the health of his young star than with records and decided to rest him. The coach's move disturbed the crowd of 46,000 who began chanting for Sayers. Halas finally relented and returned him to the lineup for the fourth quarter.

This time Sayers was inserted as a safety man for a San Francisco punt. Gale took the ball on his own 15 yard line as a phalanx of Forty-Niners approached. Sayers received the punt cleanly and began his trek to the enemy goal line, bobbing and weaving around enemy tacklers. Unbelievably, Sayers covered the muddy 85 yards as if the field was dry and fast, and scored his sixth touchdown of the day. The Bears left the field victors, 61-20, and Sayers had tied Nevers' record.

Which Players Were Involved in the Longest Match Ever Played at Wimbledon?

Charles Passarell and Pancho Gonzales, June 1969. Prior to the introduction of the tie-breaker, 25-year-old Passarell and 41-year-old Gonzales met on the center court. The match began in late afternoon and, almost immediately, there were indications that it would be a long, tense battle. Passarell enjoyed set point eleven times in the first set but couldn't score the final point. But the youngster persisted and, ultimately, won the longest set in Wimbledon history, 24-22.

Darkness was fast approaching as the second set began and, despite Gonzales' protests that the match be postponed because of poor visibility, the umpire ruled that they continue. Passarell easily won the second set, 6-1, whereupon play was suspended because of darkness after two hours and 20 minutes of play. Although he was being granted a respite, Gonzales hardly seemed able to overcome a two-set deficit.

Refreshed after a good night's sleep, Gonzales opened the third set by taking the lead from his young foe, but Pancho was unable to definitively put Passarell away. Again the match dragged on with Pancho blowing set point seven times. However, he finally prevailed, winning the set, 16-14. Inspired by the triumph, Gonzales played a calculating game in set four and took that one 6-3, to tie the match at two sets apiece.

The fifth and deciding set was a classic. Passarell moved into a commanding 5-4 lead but failed to take the clincher. Then the kid moved into a 6-5 lead but Gonzales would not waver. The old champ persisted and, as the crowd became more frenzied over the events on the grass, moved the set to a 9-9 tie.

At last the younger player began cracking under the strain; he double-faulted and hit a return out of bounds. Now Pancho was ahead, 10-9. Tasting victory, the old warrior came through to win the next game, the set, 11-9, and the match by the score of 22-24, 1-6, 16-14, 6-3, 11-9. The marathon consumed five hours and 12 minutes and a record number of games (112) were played.

Who Was the Heavyweight Champion Muhammad Ali (Then Cassius Clay) Defeated to Gain the Crown?

Sonny Liston. An unheralded underdog, Clay entered the ring in Miami on February 26, 1964, with the odds officially 8-1 against him; and for good reason. Liston had twice within a year routed onetime champion Floyd Patterson and had, in 36 attempts, knocked out 25 of his professional opponents. Apart from that Liston appeared to be in his prime and exuded a fearsome aura that often mesmerized his foes. Although Clay had won an Olympic gold medal in 1960 in the light-heavyweight class, he was not taken seriously because of his own endless *braggodocio* and flights into poetic fancy. Few critics believed that someone who boasted that he could "float like a butterfly and sting like a bee" would really do well in a crunch with the menacing Liston who said little but hit hard.

Less than 9,000 spectators turned out for the event, but those who did were instantly amazed at Clay's audacity. The challenger taunted the champ; danced around him and did, in fact, sting like a bee more often than not. Despite an eye injury, Clay persisted and so belabored the plodding Liston that, at the end of the sixth round the champion conceded the match and refused to come out for the seventh round. Clay had become the champion of the world.

Which Heavyweight Challenger Intimidated Champion Joe Louis With His "Cosmic Punch"?

Lou Nova. A devotee of yoga, Nova gained considerable publicity over his "Cosmic Punch" and supposedly revolutionary "bodily arc." The fads had their virtues, and Nova whipped no less an ace than Max Baer. However, the true test of the "Cosmic Punch" would be its ability to topple the champ of champions, Joe Louis. Amid much fuss and fanfare over Nova's "secret weapon," the champion appeared somewhat awed by the ink obtained by Nova. However, the potency of the "Cosmic Punch" was finally revealed to the public on September 29, 1941, at New York's Polo Grounds where Louis deposited Nova to the canvas with finality in the sixth round. The fight was ended at this point, and so were Nova's claims to cosmic fame.

What Was the Biggest "Steal" of Players from One League to Another Without Compensation to the "Robbed" League?

Stars of the Negro National League such as Monte Irvin, Larry Doby, and Don Newcombe made their way to the National (Irvin went to the New York Giants and Newcombe to the Brooklyn Dodgers) and American Leagues (Doby signed with the Cleveland Indians) after learning their trade for years in the black professional leagues. Yet, the white-owned major league teams refused to sufficiently compensate the leagues or teams from which stars such as Newcombe were trained.

One such black owner, Mrs. Effa Manley, tried in vain to obtain compensation from the Dodgers for Newcombe, who developed into one of major league baseball's outstanding pitchers. "I wrote to Branch Rickey (boss of the Brooklyn Dodgers)," said Mrs. Manley, "but he didn't even answer our letters, let alone give us anything. The thing was, he knew we were in no position to challenge him. We got nothing for Newcombe; $5,000 for Irvin and $15,000 for Doby; that's all. Rickey tried to take our parks, but he couldn't take them. But he did take our ballplayers. He outmaneuvered us completely."

Which Two Players Made the Greatest Catches in Baseball History?

Al Gionfriddo, Brooklyn Dodgers. Willie Mays, New York Giants. A utility outfielder, Gionfriddo executed a leaping catch in the 1947 Dodgers-New York Yankees' World Series to steal a home run away from slugger Joe DiMaggio. The catch, according to columnist Arthur Daley of *The New York Times*, was "one of the most unbelievable catches ever seen anywhere."

In the 1954 World Series, in which the Giants played the Cleveland Indians, Mays took off after an exceptionally long drive by slugger Vic Wertz at the Polo Grounds. Unlike most ball parks, the Polo Grounds had an unusually deep center-field which, in this case, benefitted Mays. Despite the enormity of Wertz's blow, the Giants' centerfielder turned his back on the ball and ran as fast as he could. At the last split second, Mays peered up and caught the ball in his glove with his back to the infield. After the game, Mays was guilty of vast overstatement when he immodestly declared: "I knew I had it all the way!"

When Was the Longest Game in National Hockey League History?

In 1935-36 the National Hockey League was still divided into two sections, a Canadian Division, which included the Montreal Maroons, Toronto Maple Leafs, New York Americans, and Montreal Canadiens, and an American Division, which included the Detroit Red Wings, Boston Bruins, Chicago Black Hawks, and New York Rangers. The Maroons finished first in the Candian Division and the Red Wings were the American Division champions. According to the system of the day, the two first-place teams would meet in the opening round of the Stanley Cup play-offs.

Judging by their respective records, which were almost identical, the Maroons and Red Wings would be in for a difficult series with bookmakers at a loss as to whom to list as the favorite. The opening game of the series at the Montreal Forum on March 24, 1936, proved how evenly matched they were.

Led by Hooley Smith, Baldy Northcott, and Jimmy Ward, the Maroons presented one of the most formidable attacks in the league. Detroit, however, was strong up front, too. The Red Wings' first line of Marty Barry, Herbie Lewis, and Larry Aurie had an impressive season with Barry winning the scoring championship in the American Division.

Despite the notable scorers on both teams three periods of play elapsed without either club scoring a goal. This meant sudden-death overtime. Although the Forum crowd was excited about the prospect of sudden death there was some reason to suspect this might be an exceptionally long night. For one thing the teams were getting excellent goaltending from Normie Smith in the Red Wing cage and Lorne Chabot of the Maroons. For another, there was precedent for a marathon match. On April 4, 1932, the Toronto Maple Leafs and Boston Bruins played past 1 A.M. in what had been the longest NHL game on record.

By the time the Maroons and Red Wings had played through the second overtime without a goal the crowd began to get restless. The players, of course, were laboring on badly chopped ice that didn't have the benefit of modern resurfacing machines in vogue today. Nevertheless, they plodded on past midnight with no end in sight.

When the sixth period began a cascade of cheers went up from the previously numbed crowd. Perhaps they hoped to inspire the Maroons to a spirited rush and a score but this didn't happen. Neither team scored and the teams moved into the seventh period as a handful of fans streamed to the exits.

Despite the hour, the majority of spectators remained in their seats. By now the monumental contest became an obsession with both players and fans and everyone seemed determined to see it through to a conclusion, no matter what happened. Nothing very much happened in the seventh period but the eighth—or fifth sudden-death—period loomed as the decisive one.

Near the end of the period Marty Barry, the Red Wings' accomplished center, was approaching collapse. With what energy he had at his command, Barry sent a pass to Herbie Lewis that catapulted his wing into the clear for a play on goal. He moved into striking distance and released a hard shot that obviously beat goalie Lorne Chabot. As Lewis prepared to raise his stick in the traditional victory salute he heard the puck clang off the goal post. It rebounded harmlessly to the corner where Hooley Smith retrieved it and began a counterattack with as much excitement as Lewis' play.

Smith was accompanied on his rush by Baldy Northcott. There was a choice, either Smith could make the play himself, using Northcott as a decoy, or he could try the pass. At first, Smith cut sharply toward the net, giving the impression he would go it alone. But, at this precise moment, he skimmed the puck to Northcott who shot hard at the Red Wing net. However, Normie Smith anticipated the play, caught the puck on his pad and steered it to teammate Doug Young who reversed the field.

Now, it appeared that each team was bent on wild kamikaze attacks in the hopes of bringing the game to a sudden end. Young raced along the boards until he reached Maroon territory. Then, he fired wildly but the puck suddenly hit Maroon defenseman Lionel Conacher's skate and changed direction, sliding straight for an empty side of the net. It appeared to be equidistant between Young and goalie Chabot. The Red Wing skater lunged for it but before he could get his stick on the rubber Chabot smothered it with his glove. Shortly thereafter the period ended and the teams had completed eight scoreless periods of play.

Four minutes and 46 seconds after the ninth period began, the teams had broken the longest-game record set by Toronto and Boston and, still, there was no end in sight. It was past 2

A.M. and many of the spectators were fighting to keep their eyes open, not wanting to miss the decisive goal if it ever was to be scored.

By this time the veterans of both teams were fatigued beyond recovery. It was essential to employ the players with the most stamina and, naturally, those with even a smidgen of energy remaining were the inexperienced younger skaters. One of them was Modere (Mud) Bruneteau, a native of St. Boniface, Manitoba, who had just one season ago played for the Wings' minor league team, the Detroit Olympics. He was the youngest man in the longest game, equipped, Jack Adams believed, with the strongest legs. Adams was the Detroit coach and he remembered, before he recently died: "The game settled into an endurance test, hour after hour. One o'clock came, and then 2 A.M., and by now the ice was a chipped, brutal mess. At 2:25 I looked along our bench for the strongest legs and I scrambled the lines to send out Syd Howe, Hec Kilrea, and Bruneteau."

As a rookie on a loaded first-place club, Bruneteau saw very little action during the season and scored only two goals while achieving no assists for a grand total of two points. But he was young and at the 12-minute mark of the ninth period, Mud Bruneteau was in a lot better shape than most of his teammates or opponents.

Adams' instructions were typically explicit. "Boys, let's get some sleep. It's now or never!"

Bruneteau surrounded the puck in the Detroit zone and passed it to Kilrea. They challenged the Montreal defense, Kilrea faking a return pass, then sliding it across the blue line. Bruneteau cut behind the defense and retrieved the puck. "Thank God," he says, "Chabot fell down as I drove it in the net. It was the funniest thing. The puck just stuck there in the twine and didn't fall on the ice."

There was a dispute when the goal judge neglected to flash his red light, but Referee Nels Stewart arbitrated. "You're bloody right it's a goal!" Stewart announced, and put up his hand as a signal. After 116 minutes and 30 seconds of overtime the Red Wings defeated the Maroons, 1-0.

There was a wild, capering anticlimax. Bruneteau's sweater was removed, not delicately, by his relieved associates. One fan thrust a $20 bill on Bruneteau as he left the ice. Other celebrants reached for their wallets. "There I was, my stick under one arm and my gloves under another, and I grabbed money in every direction!"

When he reached the Detroit dressing room, Bruneteau tossed a bundle of bills on a rubbing table. "Count it," he told Honey Walker, the trainer, "and split it for the gang." The windfall was gratifying for professionals in a depression year: $22 for each member of the Wings, including Adams, Walker, and the stickboy.

Mud Bruneteau's shot went into the net at 16:30 of the sixth overtime or 2:25 A.M. Eastern Standard Time. Normie Smith, who was playing in his first Stanley Cup game, was limp when it was over. He had stopped 90 shots in all. "We were all pretty much all in," Smith recalled years later, "but very happy."

Meanwhile, Bruneteau sat on his bed in Montreal's genteel Windsor Hotel near 5 A.M. on March 25, 1936, still unwinding from a Stanley Cup playoff that he had won for Detroit Red Wings less than three hours before. He was about to undress after a celebration when there was a knock on the door. He sat very still, not caring to be disturbed. The knocker persisted. Finally Bruneteau let his visitor in, somewhat startled to recognize the Montreal goalkeeper he had beaten to end the weary marathon. Lorne Chabot, dark eyes staring under a thicket of black brows, had come to call.

"Sorry to bother you, kid," Chabot said, "but you forgot something when you left the rink." Then, handing Bruneteau a puck, "Maybe you'd like to have this souvenir of the goal you scored."

Bruneteau, in later life operated a bar in Omaha, Nebraska. Chabot has been dead for several years. "Can you

149

imagine that such a great man as he would do such a thing for a rookie? I remember him standing there in the door. A big, handsome guy with a kind of fat-looking face. I felt, I guess, funny. He came in and we sat on the bed, and talked for a long time."

Bruneteau was a journeyman, mutely remote from stardom until one goal left him with reverberating notoriety. Afterward, apart from 35 goals scored in the wartime season of 1943-44, he was undistinguished.

"The publicity has never ended," he once said, in his Omaha oasis. "It could've happened to a lot of guys who were better players. I was just another guy named Joe."

Adams' gratification paused short of hoping prolonged games would become habitual. "Rotten ice produced rotten hockey that was torture for the players and boring for the fans. I knew the NHL had to do something."

Adams discovered what to do in the spring of 1938, when the Red Wings and Montreal Canadiens toured Europe. "I noticed one night at an ice show that the attendants swept the surface with sheepskin brushes and then flooded it before the next show." He recommended ice-flooding between periods to the NHL governors, and in 1940-41 resurfacing became mandatory. "That legislation speeded up play, because it meant the players didn't have to skate through slush late in the game. It convinced me that there'll never be any approach to Bruneteau's overtime record. There are too many shots and too much wide-open play to permit long stretches with no goals."

The impetus gained from the Red Wings' marathon opening-game win was enough to lift Detroit to a three-straight play-off victory over the Maroons and a four-game win over the Toronto Maple Leafs for the Stanley Cup. Smith, the alter hero of the marathon match, lost both trophies he had hoped to obtain as souvenirs.

His goalie stick was autographed by every member of the Red Wings but somehow wound up in the hands of a Judge John Scallen. "I also was supposed to get half the puck that was in play at the finish of the game," said Smith, "but I don't know what became of that."

Nor did he get his name inscribed in the record book that lists the longest game. That honor was bestowed on Modere (Mud) Bruneteau, the rookie who had scored only two goals all season.

Who Was the First Man to Finish the Indy 500 in Less Than 4 Hours?

Lee Wallard, driving a Belanger Special, in 1951. Wallard finished the race in 3:57:38.05, shattering the previous record by almost ten minutes.

The mark actually had been broken twice before—the first time by Davis Resta, driving a Peugeot, way back in 1916! However, the time was for 300 miles, in a shortened race. In 1950, Johnny Parsons, driving a Wynn's Special, drove across the finish line in just under 2:47. But this was an aborted race too, shortened to 345 miles by rain.

Incidentally, Wallard's average speed in that historic 1951 Indy 500, was 126.24, more than double the average speed of the first Indy winner, Ray Harroun, who won it in 1911.

Who Replaced Babe Ruth in the New York Yankees' Outfield?

George "Twinkletoes" Selkirk. In 1934, Selkirk, the son of a Huntsville, Ontario funeral director, graduated from the International League to the American League Yankees. Unlike Ruth, Selkirk was extraordinarily fast and thus earned the nickname "Twinkletoes." Although Selkirk was hardly in Ruth's class as a slugger, he was a competent fielder and steady hitter. He was twice (1936 and 1939) selected for American League All-Star teams and consistently batted at or

151

above .300. Selkirk's most commendable moment occurred at his first at-bat in the 1936 World Series when he hit a home run off the Giants' superb pitcher Carl Hubbell. When Twinkletoes' playing days were over he became a minor league manager and, later, general manager of the Washington Senators in the mid-sixties. From time to time knowledgable baseball fans would encounter Selkirk and introduce him as "the man who replaced Babe Ruth." Once, a friend so introduced Selkirk to his grandsons. The kids looked at their grandfather and replied: "Who's Babe Ruth?"